RICHARD LUNDY

TAIPEI CITY TRAVEL GUIDE 2024-2025

Exploring the Culture, Rich History and Adventure in Taiwan

This book was professionally typeset on Reedsy.
Find out more at reedsy.com

Contents

Introduction

A Brief History of Taipei

T he history of Taipei is a fascinating blend of indigenous roots, waves of migration, periods of colonial rule, and modern evolution. Here's a glimpse into its rich past:

Early Inhabitants (Before the 18th Century)

The Taipei Basin was once inhabited by the Ketagalan tribes, skilled in hunting and fishing, who thrived in the region's fertile lands and abundant resources.

18th Century: Arrival of the Han Chinese

Beginning in 1709, immigrants from mainland China, particularly from Fujian province, began settling in the area. These Han settlers established agricultural communities and a small trading post called "Mángjiǎ" (), which would later become the heart of Taipei.

19th Century: Growth and Development

By the late 19th century, Mángjiǎ had evolved into a bustling commercial centre, largely due to trade with China and the opening of the port at Tamsui (Danshui). The port's export of tea further bolstered the region's economic prominence. In 1875, Mángjiǎ became the capital of Tamsui County under the Qing dynasty's administration.

1887: The Rise of Taipei

In 1887, the Qing dynasty unexpectedly designated Mángjiǎ as the provisional capital of Taiwan province, renaming it "Táiběi" (), meaning "North of Taiwan," even though Tainan in the south was a more established settlement at the time.

1895-1945: Japanese Colonial Era

After the First Sino-Japanese War, Taiwan was ceded to Japan in 1895. Under Japanese colonial rule, Taipei experienced significant modernization and infrastructure development. Japanese influence is still evident in the city's architecture and urban design, including landmarks like the National Taiwan Museum and the Botanical Garden. Despite economic progress, there was ongoing resistance to Japanese rule among the Han Chinese population.

1945: Return to Chinese Rule

Following World War II, Taiwan was returned to Chinese control. In 1949, after the Chinese Civil War, Taipei became the provisional capital of the Republic of China (ROC) as the Kuomintang (KMT) government, led by Chiang Kai-shek, retreated from mainland China. The influx of KMT personnel and mainland refugees sparked rapid population growth and urban expansion.

Post-1949: Economic Boom and Political Transformation

Taipei became the focal point of Taiwan's remarkable economic growth during the 1950s and 1960s, spurred by land reforms, industrialization, and international trade. The 1960s and 1970s also saw the rise of Taiwan's democratic movement, which eventually led to the lifting of martial law in 1987 and the establishment of a multi-party democracy.

Today, Taipei is a bustling metropolis with a vibrant economy, rich cultural heritage, and modern infrastructure. As a global hub for technology and finance, it continues to attract international businesses and talent. While embracing progress and innovation, Taipei remains proud of its history, which is reflected in its traditional temples, lively night markets, and striking skyscrapers, a blend that perfectly captures the city's diverse character.

* * *

Why Visit Taipei in 2024-2025?

Taipei, Taiwan's vibrant capital, beckons travellers with its captivating mix of ancient traditions, modern energy, and mouth-watering cuisine. Here's why it should be your next destination:

A Culinary Wonderland
Get ready for a culinary journey: Taipei's night markets offer an array of irresistible street food, while upscale restaurants cater to refined tastes. Sample regional specialties like bubble tea and xiaolongbao, and experience a diverse food scene that promises to tantalise
your taste buds.

Rich Cultural Heritage
Step back in time: Taipei's rich cultural history is evident in its historic temples, museums brimming with ancient artefacts, and colonial-era architecture. Visit the renowned National Palace Museum, stroll through vibrant night markets steeped in tradition, and explore the city's diverse indigenous cultures.

Urban Exploration
Discover a modern metropolis: Taipei blends its historical charm with a cosmopolitan vibe. Admire the stunning views from Taipei 101, once the tallest skyscraper in the world, and explore dynamic neighbourhoods like Ximending, known for its trendy fashion and youthful energy. The city's innovative spirit and cutting-edge technology are at every turn.

Nature Retreats

Find peace in nature: Beyond its urban hustle, Taipei offers stunning natural beauty. Hike the scenic trails of Yangmingshan National Park, known for its volcanic landscapes, hot springs, and vibrant floral displays. Or, unwind at the famous Beitou Hot Springs, a serene escape from the city.

Festive Spirit

Join the festivities: Taipei loves to celebrate, and throughout the year, colourful festivals highlight Taiwan's cultural richness. Whether it's the Lantern Festival, grand temple parades, or the festive Lunar New Year, you'll find plenty of opportunities to immerse yourself in local traditions.

Warm Welcome

Experience Taiwanese hospitality: Known for their warmth and friendliness, the people of Taipei will make you feel right at home. Whether you're navigating the bustling streets or seeking local advice, expect to be greeted with smiles and genuine kindness.

In 2024-2025, Taipei promises exciting new experiences and cultural discoveries. With its dynamic development and dedication to preserving its heritage, the city offers an unforgettable adventure for travellers.

Taipei awaits with its unique blend of history, culture, adventure, and culinary delights. Let this guide help you explore this vibrant city and create lasting memories in 2024-2025.

Chapter 1: Planning Your Trip

Best Time to Visit

Taipei's subtropical climate ensures that it offers pleasant weather year-round, but the ideal time to visit depends on your preferences:

Spring (March-May)

- Pros: This is the peak tourist season, with comfortable temperatures ranging from 19-22°C (66-72°F) and the breathtaking sight of cherry blossoms, particularly in Yangmingshan National Park. It's also a season filled with numerous cultural events and festivals.

- Cons: Expect crowded attractions and higher hotel prices.

Summer (June-August)

- Pros: The hot and humid weather, with temperatures between 28-33°C (82-91°F), is great for sun-seekers and outdoor activities like exploring the lively night markets. The atmosphere is bustling with outdoor events.

- Cons: Heavy rainfall may disrupt plans, and the humidity can feel uncomfortable. Additionally, flight and accommodation prices can be slightly higher.

Fall (September–November)

- Pros: This is often considered the best time to visit Taipei, thanks to mild temperatures of 23-28°C (73-82°F) and fewer tourists. You'll find more affordable accommodation and stunning autumn foliage, especially at Yangmingshan National Park.

- Cons: September can be typhoon season, so it's important to keep an eye on weather forecasts. Some events might not take place during this period.

Winter (December–February)

- Pros: With mild weather (13-18°C/55-64°F) and fewer tourists, winter offers a peaceful and affordable experience. The festive atmosphere during Christmas and Lunar New Year celebrations adds to the charm.

- Cons: Some outdoor attractions may have limited hours or closures. You may also encounter occasional cold fronts and grey skies.

Special Events
Consider planning your visit around these exciting events:
1. Taipei Lantern Festival (February): A magical display of lanterns lighting

up the city.

2. Double Ten National Day (October 10th): A vibrant celebration of Taiwan's National Day.

3. Taipei International Dragon Boat Festival (June): Thrilling dragon boat races combined with cultural performances.

Ultimately, your ideal time to visit depends on your priorities:

1. Spring or fall for mild weather and festivals.
2. Summer for outdoor fun despite the heat.
3. Winter for budget-friendly travel and fewer crowds.

* * *

Budgeting for Your Trip

Taipei offers a fantastic range of experiences that won't break the bank. Here's a guide to help you budget for your 2024-2025 trip, based on your travel style and tips to save money:

Know Your Travel Style
  1. Luxury: Spend $250 USD or more per day for high-end hotels, gourmet dining, and exclusive experiences.

2. Mid-Range: Allocate $100-$150 USD daily for boutique hotels, local restaurants, and paid attractions.

3. Budget: You can manage $50-$80 USD per day by staying in hostels, eating street food, and enjoying free attractions.

Accommodation

1. Options: Taipei offers everything from luxury hotels to budget-friendly hostels. Choose a location that's both convenient and cost-effective.

2. Cost: Hostel dorm beds start at $20-$30 USD per night, budget hotels range from $40-$60 USD, and mid-range hotels typically cost $80-$120 USD.

Food

1. Variety: Enjoy street food for $2-$5 USD per dish, local restaurants for meals costing $8-$15 USD, and fine dining from $30-$100+ USD.

2. Saving Tips: Opt for street food, look for lunch specials, and pack snacks to save on dining costs.

Transportation

1. Public Transit: The affordable MRT, buses, and taxis make getting around easy. Consider getting an EasyCard for convenience.

2. Cost: MRT tickets range from $1.50-$3.50 USD, and daily passes are available. Taxis operate on metres.

Activities and Attractions

1. Free Fun: Visit temples, night markets, parks, and free museums.

2. Paid Experiences: Set aside money for popular attractions like the National Palace Museum or the Taipei 101 observation deck.

Additional Costs

1. Insurance: Don't forget to factor in travel insurance.

2. Souvenirs: Budget for local crafts and souvenirs.

3. Entertainment: Allocate funds for nightlife and other leisure activities.

Saving Tips

1. Off-Season: Travel in spring or fall to avoid peak prices.

2. Walk: Explore the city on foot to save on transportation.

3. Free Activities: Prioritise free experiences like parks and temples.

4. Cook: Prepare some of your own meals to cut dining costs.

5. Learn Mandarin: Basic Mandarin can help you communicate better and possibly save money by avoiding tourist traps.

* * *

Packing Essentials for Taipei

Taipei's subtropical climate varies throughout the year, so packing wisely ensures a comfortable trip. Here's a guide to what you'll need:

General Essentials

1. Comfortable Walking Shoes: Choose shoes with good support and traction for walking the city's streets and night markets.

2. Lightweight, Breathable Clothing: Cotton or linen fabrics work well for most seasons. Layers are helpful for temperature changes.

3. Quick-Drying Clothes: Humidity and occasional rain make quick-dry fabrics a good choice.

4. Reusable Water Bottle: Stay hydrated and reduce plastic use.

5. Umbrella or Light Raincoat: Spring and summer showers are frequent.

6. Sunscreen, Hat, and Sunglasses: The sun can be strong year-round.

7. Adapter Plug: Taipei uses Type A and B plugs, with a standard voltage of 110V.

8. Currency Converter App (Optional): Helpful for quick currency conversions.

9. Small First-Aid Kit: Basic medical supplies for any minor incidents.

10. Toiletries: Travel-sized versions help save space.

Seasonal Considerations

1. Spring (March-May): Bring layers for varying temperatures, plus rain gear for unpredictable showers.

2. Summer (June-August): Pack lightweight, breathable clothes, sun protection, and insect repellent.

3. Autumn (September-November): Comfortable clothing for mild weather, plus a light jacket for cooler evenings.

4. Winter (December-February): Light jackets, sweaters, and a scarf for chilly nights.

Additional Considerations

1. Formal Events: Bring one dressier outfit for any formal occasions.

2. Temple Etiquette: A light scarf or sarong can cover shoulders during temple visits.

3. Hiking: Pack proper hiking shoes and breathable outdoor clothing if you plan on exploring nature.

4. Night Markets: Evenings can get cool, so consider bringing a light jacket or sweater.

* * *

Transportation Options in Taipei

Taipei boasts an efficient and affordable public transportation system, making it easy to get around the city. Here's a breakdown of your options:

The Unbeatable Taipei MRT

1. Efficient Connectivity: The Taipei Metro (MRT) system connects all major districts and attractions with over 130 stations on five lines.

2. User-Friendly: Stations and signage are clear, with information in both English and Mandarin. Ticket machines are multilingual and easy to use.

3. Cost-Effective: MRT fares are affordable. Get an EasyCard for seamless travel and discounts.

4. Accessibility: The MRT system is disability-friendly, with elevators, ramps, and tactile paving at most stations.

Exploring by Bus

1. Extensive Network: The bus system complements the MRT, covering areas that the metro doesn't reach.

2. Planning: Routes can be tricky to navigate at first, but apps and friendly locals can help you find your way.

3. Payment: Pay bus fares using either cash or the EasyCard.

Taxis and Ride-Sharing
   1. Convenient: Taxis and ride-sharing apps like Uber are readily available and ideal for shorter trips or late-night travel.

2. Communication: Many drivers may not speak English, so having your destination written in Mandarin or using a translation app can be helpful.

YouBike: Exploring at Your Own Pace
   1. Eco-Friendly: YouBike is a public bicycle-sharing system, perfect for short-term exploration.
   2. Affordable: Rates are budget-friendly, and docking stations are conveniently located throughout the city.

Additional Options
   1. Airport MRT: Direct service connects Taipei City with Taoyuan International Airport.

2. High-Speed Rail (HSR): The HSR links Taipei with major cities across Taiwan, making intercity travel fast and convenient.

Tips for Choosing Transportation
   1. Consider Distance: Use the MRT for longer trips, and buses for shorter distances or areas not served by the metro.

2. Luggage: If you have bulky luggage, taxis or ride-sharing may be more

convenient than public transit.

3. Time: Avoid peak hours on the MRT, or consider YouBike during busy periods.

With these essentials and transportation options in mind, your trip to Taipei will be smooth and enjoyable, no matter the season.

Chapter 2: Exploring Taipei's Neighbourhoods

Xinyi District

X inyi District represents the cutting-edge of modern Taipei, with towering skyscrapers, luxury malls, and high-end business centres. It's a neighbourhood that showcases the city's forward-thinking spirit, blending opulence with innovation.

At its heart stands Taipei 101, an iconic symbol of Taipei's modernization. Visitors can ascend to its observation deck for awe-inspiring panoramic views of the city. The nearby Taipei Nangang Exhibition Center hosts international conventions, further establishing Xinyi as a global business hub.

Luxury Shopping

Xinyi is synonymous with upscale shopping. The Taipei 101 Mall features prestigious international brands, while Shin Kong Place One and Pacific Sogo Department Store house an array of designer boutiques.

Art and Culture

Xinyi is also a hub for the arts. Venues like Eslite Spectrum Taipei and the Miramar Foundation Art Center offer contemporary art exhibitions, making it a vibrant cultural destination.

Dining

Xinyi caters to all culinary tastes, from Michelin-starred restaurants to casual eateries. Whether you're looking for high-end international cuisine or hidden local gems, you'll find it here.

Nightlife

The district's nightlife is just as sophisticated. Rooftop bars and upscale clubs offer stunning city views, with live music and handcrafted cocktails adding to the elegant atmosphere.

Planning Your Visit

Xinyi is easily accessible via Taipei's MRT system, with stations like Taipei 101 and City Hall connecting you to the heart of the district. Even on a budget, you can enjoy window shopping, admiring the district's modern architecture, or sampling its delicious street food.

* * *

Datong District

Datong District, located in eastern Taipei, may be small, but its historical significance is monumental. As the birthplace of Taipei's story, it's a treasure trove for history enthusiasts and cultural explorers.

Dadaocheng

Step into the past by visiting Dadaocheng, the heart of Datong and Taipei's oldest commercial hub. Walk through narrow streets lined with traditional shops offering everything from tea to artisanal crafts. The well-preserved Baroque-style buildings here are remnants of the Qing Dynasty. Don't miss Dadaocheng Wharf, a landmark that has witnessed Taipei's transformation from a humble port town to a thriving urban centre.

Temples and Traditions

Datong is a spiritual haven. Visit the majestic Longshan Temple, a blend of Buddhist and Taoist influences adorned with intricate designs. Another must-see is the Confucius Temple, a tribute to the revered philosopher and a window into Taiwan's cultural heritage.

Modern Transformation

Datong has embraced the modern era while maintaining its historical roots. This evolution is evident in trendy cafes and art galleries that now sit alongside traditional establishments. Red Hall 1914, a revitalised Japanese-era market, is now a cultural hotspot featuring art displays, boutique shops, and stylish eateries. Dihua Street is another highlight, offering a sensory experience of dried goods, spices, and traditional remedies.

Night Market Indulgence

A visit to Datong wouldn't be complete without experiencing its vibrant street food scene. Head to Wanhua Night Market to savour local Taiwanese delicacies like oyster omelettes, stinky tofu, and bubble tea.

Datong's Secrets

To uncover the district's hidden gems, explore the charming Beimen area, with its traditional shops and cosy eateries. Take a peaceful stroll along the Tamsui River, providing a serene escape from the city's hustle and bustle.

Where to Stay

Datong offers a range of accommodation options, from boutique hotels housed in historic buildings to budget-friendly hostels ideal for meeting fellow travellers. You can also find modern hotels equipped with all the comforts for a relaxing stay.

* * *

Zhongshan District

In the centre of Taipei, Zhongshan District blends historical charm with contemporary flair and a flourishing culinary scene. This vibrant area offers a snapshot of Taipei's essence, showcasing everything from ancient temples to cutting-edge art galleries and gourmet dining.

Heritage and History

Zhongshan District boasts significant historical landmarks, including the intricately designed Longshan Temple, a symbol of Buddhist and Taoist traditions. Take a stroll through Dadaocheng, once a bustling trade centre, where Qing dynasty architecture still stands as a testament to Taipei's rich past.

Gastronomic Delights

The district is a paradise for food lovers. Raohe Street Night Market is a must-visit for street food, with a wide variety of Taiwanese delicacies. Beyond the bustling market scene, Zhongshan is home to Michelin-starred restaurants and hidden gems that offer everything from renowned xiao long bao at Din Tai Fung to flavorful Hakka cuisine.

Shopping and Art

Zhongshan is also a hub for trendsetters. Fashion-forward shoppers can explore Zhongshan North Road, home to both local and international designer boutiques. The district's thriving art scene features contemporary galleries and intimate studios, perfect for art enthusiasts looking to discover the latest trends.

Hidden Gems

For a more tranquil experience, escape to the greenery of Xinsheng Park, a peaceful retreat popular with locals. History buffs can explore Taiwan's cinematic heritage at the Taipei Film House, or marvel at intricate displays at the Miniatures Museum of Taiwan.

Accessibility and Accommodation

Zhongshan's central location makes it easy to reach by public transportation, with multiple MRT stations providing convenient connections to other parts of Taipei. The district offers a wide range of accommodation options, from luxurious five-star hotels to charming boutique guesthouses, making it an ideal base for exploring the city.

* * *

Wanhua District

As Taipei's oldest neighbourhood, Wanhua District pulses with history and culture, offering visitors a glimpse into the city's storied past while embracing the energy of the present.

A Window into the Past

Wanhua's history stretches back centuries as the birthplace of Taipei. The district is filled with historic landmarks, from ancient temples to narrow alleys that preserve the city's heritage. At the heart of Wanhua stands Longshan Temple, a masterpiece of Buddhist and Taoist architecture dating back to the 18th century. This iconic temple is a spiritual and cultural landmark that continues to draw visitors seeking to experience Taiwanese religious customs.

Bopiliao Historical Block

Another key highlight is the Bopiliao Historical Block, where red-brick buildings from Taipei's past have been meticulously preserved. This area, once a thriving commercial centre, now houses art galleries, teahouses, and cafes, offering a glimpse into Wanhua's rich architectural legacy.

Ximending

In the northern part of Wanhua, Ximending stands as a vibrant hub of youth culture, often referred to as the "Harajuku of Taipei." This area is packed with clothing stores, indie boutiques, and street art, making it a hotspot for fashion enthusiasts. Red House Theater, a cultural icon, offers performances and a glimpse into Taipei's artistic history. Ximending's bustling energy is complemented by a variety of street food options, perfect for indulging in local flavours.

Night Market Extravaganza

Wanhua is also famous for its night markets, including Snake Alley, where adventurous eaters can sample snake-inspired dishes, and Huaxi Street Night Market, which offers a mix of traditional Taiwanese treats and international flavours.

Exploring Hidden Treasures

Beyond the main attractions, Wanhua has hidden gems waiting to be discovered. Dihua Street is a bustling market filled with dried goods, herbal remedies, and traditional crafts, while Baoan Temple Lane offers a quieter, more spiritual experience with historic shrines nestled along picturesque lanes.

Accommodation and Accessibility

Wanhua District caters to all types of travellers with its diverse lodging options, from budget-friendly guesthouses to boutique hotels housed in heritage buildings. The district is easily accessible by public transportation, with MRT lines and buses connecting it seamlessly to the rest of Taipei.

* * *

Da'an District

Da'an District, aptly named for "great safety" or "great peace," offers a unique balance of urban vibrancy and serene tranquillity. This coveted district is a cultural and educational hub while also serving as a peaceful retreat for residents and visitors.

Cultural and Educational Haven

At the heart of Da'an is National Taiwan University (NTU), one of Taiwan's most prestigious institutions. The area buzzes with a lively student community, infusing it with youthful energy, evident in the abundance of cafes, bookshops, and trendy boutiques that cater to their tastes. Art lovers can explore cultural treasures such as the National Taiwan University Hospital Historical Museum, which delves into Taiwan's medical history, or visit contemporary art galleries showcasing local talent.

Green Oasis Amidst the City

Da'an is also home to Da'an Forest Park, a sprawling green space often referred to as the "lungs of Taipei." This lush urban park offers a peaceful escape with scenic walking trails, tranquil lakes, and open spaces perfect for relaxation. Visitors can rent paddle boats, enjoy bird-watching, or simply unwind in this verdant haven.

Culinary Extravaganza

Food enthusiasts will be spoiled for choice in Da'an. From Michelin-starred restaurants to cosy local eateries, the district's culinary offerings are as diverse as they are delightful. Whether you're craving authentic Taiwanese flavours or eager to explore international cuisines, Da'an restaurants cater to every palate.

Nightlife with a Sophisticated Twist

Da'an nightlife scene is more refined compared to the bustling energy of Ximending. Here, you'll find upscale bars, chic pubs, and stylish cocktail lounges offering a more elegant and relaxed evening experience.

Retail Therapy for Every Taste

Whether you're seeking luxury brands or hunting for unique finds, Da'an has something for every shopper. Upscale boutiques and independent designer stores line the streets, while Gongguan Night Market offers trendy, budget-friendly fashion and delicious street food.

Accommodation Options

Da'an provides a range of accommodation options, from luxurious five-star hotels to boutique guesthouses. Whether you're seeking opulence or cosy comfort, you're sure to find the perfect spot to rest after a day of exploring.

Convenient Connectivity

Da'an District is well-connected, with multiple MRT stations making it easy to travel across Taipei. The area's excellent public transportation network, including taxis and ride-hailing services, ensures you can explore Taipei with ease.

Must-See Attractions

1. National Taiwan University
2. Da'an Forest Park
3. Gongguan Night Market
4. National Taiwan University Hospital Historical Museum
5. Trendy shops, cafes, and restaurants along Da'an Road and Ren'ai Road

* * *

Beitou District

In the foothills of Yangmingshan National Park, Beitou District offers a serene sanctuary just a short distance from Taipei's bustling urban core. Known for its natural hot springs and rich heritage, Beitou has long been cherished for its rejuvenating atmosphere and scenic beauty.

Natural Hot Springs

Beitou's famous hot springs are its main draw, attracting visitors seeking to experience the therapeutic benefits of the mineral-rich waters. Whether you opt for a traditional Japanese-style ryokan or a luxurious modern spa, soaking in the hot springs with views of the surrounding mountains is an unparalleled experience.

Beitou Hot Spring Museum

For an insightful look into the history of Taiwan's hot springs, visit the Beitou Hot Spring Museum. Once a public bathhouse, this beautifully restored building now houses exhibits on Taiwan's hot spring culture and the history of Beitou as a spa destination.

Beyond the Springs

1. Thermal Valley: Witness one of nature's wonders at Thermal Valley, where steam rises from the earth in an otherworldly display of geothermal activity. Observation decks offer stunning views of this unique natural phenomenon.

2. Beitou Park: Enjoy the tranquillity of Beitou Park, where traditional Chinese gardens, winding paths, and serene ponds create a peaceful environment perfect for a leisurely stroll.

3. Beitou Public Library: Architecture enthusiasts will appreciate the Beitou Public Library, a striking example of green design that seamlessly blends with its natural surroundings.

Historic Charms

Beitou's heritage is reflected in landmarks like the Beitou Historic Station, a quaint railway station that serves as a reminder of the district's transportation history. Plum Garden, another historical gem, is known for its beautiful plum blossoms and serene ambiance.

Adventurous Explorations

Beitou serves as the gateway to Yangmingshan National Park, where outdoor enthusiasts can explore scenic hiking trails, volcanic landscapes, and vibrant seasonal blooms. For a deeper dive into local culture, visit the Beitou Museum, which showcases Beitou's history, or enjoy a traditional tea ceremony at one of the district's teahouses.

Culinary Delights

After a day of exploration, indulge in Beitou's diverse culinary offerings. The district is known for Japanese-inspired hot pot dishes and fresh seafood, while traditional tea ceremonies provide a peaceful way to unwind.

Convenient Connectivity

Beitou is easily accessible via Taipei's MRT system, with Beitou Station serving as the terminal stop on the red line. This convenient access makes it easy to visit Beitou for a day trip or longer stay.

Must-See Attractions

1. Beitou Hot Springs
2. Thermal Valley
3. Beitou Hot Spring Museum
4. Beitou Park

5. Yangmingshan National Park
6. Beitou Public Library
7. Plum Garden

* * *

Songshan District

Songshan District, located in northeastern Taipei, is a captivating blend of history, culture, and modernity, offering visitors a diverse array of experiences. Once known as "Sikou" by the indigenous Ketagalan people, Songshan has transformed from a hunting and fishing haven into one of Taipei's most vibrant financial and cultural centers.

Legacy of "Sikou"

Songshan's journey through history is marked by significant changes, especially during the Japanese colonial period when the area transitioned from tea production to becoming an administrative and commercial hub. After World War II, Songshan grew into a pivotal financial centre, with towering skyscrapers along Dunhua North Road and Nanjing East Road, housing prominent financial institutions and corporate offices.

Cultural Oasis

1. Raohe Street Night Market: A visit to Songshan wouldn't be complete without exploring the famous Raohe Street Night Market. This bustling market is a sensory delight, offering a wide variety of street food, local crafts, and an electric atmosphere that showcases the essence of Taipei's night market culture.

2. Songshan Cultural and Creative Park: Step into a world of creativity and history at the Songshan Cultural and Creative Park. Housed in the former Songshan Tobacco Factory, this cultural hub hosts art exhibitions, cultural events, and offers a glimpse into the past while promoting modern creative industries. The park's historical charm and vibrant cultural scene make it a must-visit destination.

3. Ciyou Temple: For a moment of tranquillity, visit Ciyou Temple, a majestic Buddhist sanctuary. The temple's intricate architecture and peaceful ambiance provide a serene escape from the city's bustle while offering insight into Taiwan's spiritual traditions.

Culinary Scene

While the Raohe Street Night Market is the star of Songshan's culinary landscape, the district offers much more than street food. Explore hidden cafes, upscale dining establishments, and local eateries serving authentic Taiwanese cuisine. Whether you're craving classic night market snacks or a more refined dining experience, Songshan has something to satisfy every palate.

Convenient Connectivity

Songshan Airport makes it easy for travellers to access Taipei, especially for domestic flights. The district is also well-served by Taipei's efficient public transportation system, with MRT lines and buses providing convenient access to Songshan's many attractions.

Must-See Attractions

1. Raohe Street Night Market
2. Songshan Cultural and Creative Park
3. Ciyou Temple
4. Dunhua North Road and Nanjing East Road financial district

Chapter 3: Must-Visit Attractions

National Palace Museum

The National Palace Museum in Taipei is a stunning tribute to Taiwanese heritage, displaying an extraordinary collection of Chinese imperial artefacts and art. With over 698,856 pieces spanning nearly 5,000 years, it offers a fascinating glimpse into China's artistic and cultural evolution.

Exploring the Collection

The museum's vast collection boasts a wide range of treasures, including:

1. Paintings: From the Song to the Qing dynasties, the museum showcases masterpieces that capture the progression of Chinese painting, featuring everything from majestic landscapes to detailed portraits.

2. Calligraphy: Discover the beauty of Chinese calligraphy, where characters turn into art, highlighting the elegant strokes of respected calligraphers.

3. Jade Artefacts: Admire the intricate craftsmanship of jade carvings, prized for their beauty and cultural importance throughout Chinese history.

4. Ceramics: Dive into the world of Chinese ceramics, with exhibits ranging from delicate porcelain to richly decorated pottery.

5. Bronzes: Explore ancient Chinese bronze casting through an impressive selection of sculptures, vessels, and weaponry.

6. Precious Materials: Enjoy a dazzling array of objects crafted from jadeite, lacquerware, textiles, and more, each representing the height of craftsmanship.

Navigating the Museum

With such a vast collection, making the most of your visit is key. Here are some tips:

1. Thematic Exhibitions: The museum regularly hosts exhibitions that focus on specific eras, themes, or artists. Check the website to find those that interest you.

2. Audio Guides: Enrich your visit with in-depth commentary on select items, available in multiple languages for rent.

3. Guided Tours: Join a guided tour in English or other languages to explore the museum's highlights with the help of an expert.

Planning Your Visit

1. Location: The museum is situated in the Shilin District and is easily accessible via MRT and buses.

2. Opening Hours: Generally open daily, but it's a good idea to check the website for any changes, especially on Mondays.

3. Admission Fees: Admission is charged, with discounts for students, seniors, and groups. If you plan on visiting multiple Taipei museums, consider purchasing a multi-day pass.

Other Attractions

1. Palace Grounds: Take a leisurely stroll through the peaceful gardens and courtyards, offering a quiet break from the city's hustle and bustle.

2. Theatrical Performances: Watch out for traditional Chinese performances that occasionally take place on-site.

3. Museum Shops: Explore the gift shops for unique souvenirs and replicas of the museum's treasures.

* * *

Chiang Kai-shek Memorial Hall

Located on the eastern side of Memorial Hall Park in Taipei, the Chiang Kai-shek Memorial Hall stands as a significant national symbol, providing insight into Taiwan's complex history.

Built in memory of Chiang Kai-shek, the former president of the Republic of China (ROC), this grand structure commemorates his legacy and the Kuomintang (KMT) party's rule in Taiwan. Construction began in 1976, following President Chiang's death, and was completed in 1980.

Architect Yang Cho-cheng designed the memorial to incorporate traditional Chinese architectural elements, drawing inspiration from the Sun Yat-sen Mausoleum in Nanjing, China. The hall, made of white marble, features a striking main chamber topped with a blue-glazed roof that mirrors the colors of the ROC flag.

One of the highlights is the daily changing of the guard ceremony, performed with military precision in the plaza in front of the memorial hall, reflecting timeless tradition.

Inside the main hall, you'll find a grand bronze statue of Chiang Kai-shek, with its gaze symbolically directed towards mainland China.

The hall also houses permanent and temporary exhibits that explore Chiang Kai-shek's life, the history of the KMT, and Taiwan's political journey.

Next to the memorial hall are the National Theater and National Concert Hall, which, together with the memorial, form the National Chiang Kai-shek Cultural Center. These venues regularly host cultural performances and events.

Surrounding the memorial is Memorial Hall Park, a peaceful green space ideal for relaxing walks, picnics, and enjoying nature.

Planning Your Visit
1. Hours: Open daily from 9:00 am to 6:00 pm, with free admission.

2. Other Attractions: Enhance your visit by checking out the nearby National Theater and National Concert Hall or unwinding in Memorial Hall Park.

3. Changing of the Guard: The guard-changing ceremony takes place daily at 1:00 pm.

Historical Context
Though the memorial honours Chiang Kai-shek and the KMT's rule in Taiwan, it's important to recognize the complexities of this period. To gain a deeper understanding of Taiwan's history, consider visiting the National 228 Memorial Museum, which sheds light on the 228 Incident, a time of political turmoil during KMT rule.

* * *

Longshan Temple

Among Taipei's high-rise buildings and bustling streets, Longshan Temple (, Lóngshān Sì) offers a peaceful retreat and is a must-see destination for cultural exploration in 2024-2025.

Founded in 1738, Longshan Temple has witnessed Taipei's transformation. Originally a sanctuary dedicated to Guanyin, the Goddess of Mercy, it has since evolved into a spiritual center honoring a diverse range of deities, reflecting the city's rich religious heritage.

Longshan Temple is a stunning blend of architectural styles. The main hall, with its intricate roof carvings and vibrant colors, showcases traditional Southern Chinese design, while touches of Japanese and Baroque influences add a unique twist.

As visitors step through the grand entrance, they are welcomed by a serene courtyard featuring incense burners and detailed sculptures of mythical creatures and Buddhist symbols.

Inside the main hall, a magnificent statue of Guanyin stands alongside numerous other celestial figures, representing various teachings of Buddhism.

Exploring the side halls, which are dedicated to deities such as Mazu and the Medicine Buddha, offers a deeper understanding of Taiwanese Buddhism. Each hall has its own distinctive atmosphere and sacred objects.

Cultural Significance

Throughout the year, Longshan Temple comes alive with religious ceremonies and vibrant festivals that attract both worshippers and visitors. Participating in these events offers a unique opportunity to experience local customs and connect with Taiwan's cultural roots.

Practical Information

1. Location: Found at the intersection of Bade Rd. Sec. 1 and Guangzhou St. in the Bangka and Wanhua Districts.

2. Opening Hours: Open daily from 7:30 am to 5:30 pm.

3. Admission: Free of charge.

4. Dress Code: Although not strictly enforced, it is recommended to dress modestly, with shoulders and knees covered, out of respect for the sacred space.

* * *

Taipei 101

Taipei 101, once known as the Taipei World Financial Center, stands as a symbol of modern Taipei. It's a must-visit for travelers seeking breathtaking views, cutting-edge architecture, and an insight into the city's vibrant spirit.

Soaring to 508.2 meters (1,667 feet), Taipei 101 was the tallest building in the world from its completion in 2004 until 2009. Even today, it remains Taiwan's tallest skyscraper and ranks as the 11th tallest globally.

The design of Taipei 101 draws inspiration from traditional pagodas, combining symbolism with functionality. Its segmented exterior resembles bamboo, a symbol of resilience and growth in Chinese culture. The building's advanced engineering ensures it can withstand earthquakes and typhoons, making it a remarkable feat of modern construction.

One of the main attractions of Taipei 101 is the stunning views it offers. Visitors can ascend to the observation decks on the 88th and 89th floors, where they are treated to panoramic views of the sprawling city below. On clear days, the mountains and coastline in the distance enhance the experience.

A Multi-Dimensional Experience

In addition to the breathtaking views, Taipei 101 offers a variety of experiences:

1. Observatory Exploration: Discover interactive exhibits and multimedia presentations that explain the building's construction and cultural significance.

2. Damper Tour: See the world's largest tuned mass damper, an engineering marvel that helps stabilise the tower during extreme weather.

3. Gastronomic Delights: Savour gourmet meals at one of the upscale restaurants within the complex, where the food is as impressive as the panoramic city views.

4. Retail Therapy: Explore the luxurious shopping mall at the tower's base, which offers a mix of international brands and local boutiques.

Planning Your Excursion

1. Location: Located in Taipei City's lively Xinyi District and easily accessible by public transportation.

2. Opening Hours: Generally open from 9:00 am to 10:00 pm, though hours may vary depending on the season.

3. Tickets: Tickets can be purchased online or at the ticket counter. During peak times, consider opting for express tickets to skip the lines.

* * *

Shilin Night Market

A trip to Taipei isn't complete without experiencing the lively atmosphere of a night market, and Shilin Night Market is the quintessential destination. This expansive market is a sensory delight, with an array of vendors that promise to captivate your taste buds and engage your senses.

Shilin Night Market boasts an impressive variety of culinary offerings, show-casing Taiwan's rich food culture. From classic dishes like stinky tofu and oyster omelettes to adventurous options such as snake soup and pig's blood cake, there's something to satisfy every palate. Don't miss out on popular Taiwanese treats like bubble tea, scallion pancakes, and crispy fried chicken. It's a true feast for food lovers.

Beyond the food, the market provides a diverse cultural experience. Stalls offer clothing, accessories, and souvenirs, making it a great place for both bargain hunting and souvenir shopping. Engage in some haggling and soak in the vibrant market atmosphere, filled with lively sights, sounds, and smells.

Tips for Enjoying Shilin Night Market
1. Comfortable Shoes: Wear comfortable footwear and be prepared for crowds, especially between 7 pm and 10 pm.

2. Cash: Bring cash, as many vendors may not accept credit cards.

3. Be Adventurous: Try new flavours and dishes. Basic Mandarin phrases or pointing at pictures can help with communication.

4. Watch Your Belongings: Keep an eye on your possessions in the crowded market.

Getting There

Take the MRT (Mass Rapid Transit) Red Line to Shilin Station. Exit 1 will lead you directly to the market.

Opening Hours

The market usually operates from 5 pm to midnight, though some vendors may stay open later.

* * *

Elephant Mountain

Elephant Mountain, or Xiangshan Hiking Trail, is a must-visit spot in Taipei, offering a delightful mix of natural beauty and stunning urban views. Here's how to make the most of your visit:

Why Visit

1. Panoramic Views: The summit of Elephant Mountain provides breathtaking 360-degree views of Taipei City, with Taipei 101 prominently in the skyline.

2. Easy Access: The hike is relatively short and manageable, taking about 20-30 minutes to reach the top, making it accessible to various fitness levels.

3. Natural Escape: Enjoy a break from the city's hustle as you wander through lush greenery and fresh air.

Planning Your Visit

1. Location: Elephant Mountain is located in the Xinyi District, close to Taipei 101.

2. Getting There: Take the MRT to Xiangshan Station (Exit 2) and follow the signs to the Xiangshan Hiking Trail.

3. Opening Hours: The trail is accessible at all hours, but daylight is preferable for safety and optimal views. Sunrise and sunset are particularly special times to visit.

4. What to Bring: Wear sturdy, comfortable shoes for uneven terrain. Bring sun protection like a hat and sunscreen for daytime visits, and a light jacket for cooler weather.

Tips for Your Visit

1. Arrive Early: To avoid crowds, especially on weekends and holidays, try to visit early.

2. Trail Etiquette: Maintain a steady pace and keep noise to a minimum to preserve the tranquillity of the trail.

3. Photography Tips: Use a wide-angle lens to capture the expansive cityscape and consider bringing a tripod for stable, long-exposure shots.

Extend your visit by exploring nearby attractions like Taipei 101 or the upscale venues in the Xinyi District.

* * *

Yangmingshan National Park

Yangmingshan National Park, located within the natural beauty of Taipei, offers a peaceful retreat from the city's fast pace. Shaped by ancient volcanic activity, the park features a diverse landscape, including lush mountains, green valleys, hot springs, and steaming vents. Visitors can explore its geological wonders by hiking through volcanic craters, admiring unique rock formations, and breathing in the characteristic sulfuric scent in the air.

The park offers a variety of hiking trails suitable for all levels. Adventurous hikers can challenge themselves by climbing to the top of Qixing Mountain, the park's highest peak, where breathtaking views of the Taipei Basin await. For a more relaxed experience, visitors can wander along scenic paths lined with colorful flowers, especially during the beautiful spring and autumn seasons.

Yangmingshan is also famous for its hot springs, where visitors can soak in mineral-rich waters known for their healing properties. Whether in natural hot springs or modern spa facilities, the warm waters provide relaxation and rejuvenation. Beitou Hot Springs, located at the base of the park, is a particularly popular spot for unwinding.

The park's scenery transforms with the seasons. In spring, cherry and plum blossoms create a pink and white landscape. Summer brings a blanket of greenery, offering a cool escape from the city's heat. Autumn sets the park ablaze with vibrant foliage, and in winter, a rare dusting of snow adds a magical touch.

Cultural and historical sites are also scattered throughout Yangmingshan. Visitors can admire the whimsical Yangmingshan National Park Flower Clock, decorated with seasonal flowers, and learn about the area's hot spring heritage at the Beitou Hot Springs Museum.

Planning Your Visit

Yangmingshan is easily accessible from Taipei City by public buses and taxis. A Taipei Fun Pass can be a great option for discounted transportation within the park. Guided hikes and tours are available for those interested in learning more about the park's ecology and geology.

Beitou Hot Springs

Tucked away in a tranquil valley near Yangmingshan National Park, Beitou Hot Springs offers a perfect escape from Taipei's urban life.

Here's why Beitou Hot Springs is worth a visit

1. Natural Wonders: Formed by geothermal activity, Beitou's hot springs are rich in minerals, especially sulphur, known for their therapeutic benefits. These waters are celebrated for their ability to relax muscles, improve circulation, and enhance overall health.

2. Relaxation and Renewal: Soothe your senses in Beitou's warm, mineral-rich waters. Whether you choose a public bathhouse or a private resort, the experience promises deep relaxation, and traditional spa treatments can further enhance your visit.

3. Historical Significance: Explore Beitou's history at the Beitou Hot Spring Museum, located in a charming Japanese-style building. The museum showcases the ancient bathing traditions and cultural importance of hot springs in the region.

4. Variety of Experiences: Beitou offers something for everyone, from luxurious resorts with private baths to traditional public bathhouses like the Beitou Hot Spring Public Recreation Center. Some public baths even have outdoor pools with stunning views.

5. Easy Access: Just a short MRT ride from Taipei City, Beitou Hot Springs is an ideal spot for a day trip or a peaceful overnight stay.

Exploring Beitou Hot Springs

1. Public vs. Private: Choose between the communal atmosphere of public bathhouses and the privacy of exclusive resorts, depending on your preferences and budget.

2. Beyond Bathing: Discover Beitou's historic district, featuring quaint Japanese architecture and charming shops. Visit Hell Valley to see the geothermal marvels of boiling pools and steaming vents, or take a scenic hike and enjoy views from a cable car.

Tips for Your Visit

1. Plan Ahead: Decide whether you want a public or private experience and research your options. Consider making reservations in advance, especially for popular resorts during busy times.

2. Pack Essentials: Bring swimwear, towels, slippers, and toiletries. While public bathhouses provide some amenities, it's wise to have your own.

3. Respect Local Customs: Shower before entering the hot springs and be mindful of etiquette in communal areas.

4. Protect the Environment: Help preserve Beitou's natural beauty by avoiding harsh soaps in the hot springs and disposing of waste properly.

Beitou Hot Springs offer a blend of relaxation, history, and natural beauty. Whether you seek luxury or tradition, a visit to Beitou provides a memorable retreat in the heart of Taipei's vibrant landscape.

* * *

Ximending

Often referred to as the "Harajuku of Taipei," Ximending is a vibrant district brimming with youthful energy, fashionable trends, and a buzzing nightlife, making it a must-visit spot for those exploring Taipei. Here's what to look forward to in this lively area:

1. Pedestrian Paradise: Wander through the lively pedestrian zone, where narrow streets are filled with shops, arcades, and bustling street vendors, creating an immersive urban experience.

2. Shopping Spree: Satisfy your shopping desires by exploring trendy boutiques offering the latest fashion, independent stores with unique finds, and department stores catering to all budgets and tastes.

3. Culinary Adventure: Indulge in a variety of Taiwanese delicacies and international dishes. From affordable street snacks like bubble tea and oyster omelettes to chic cafes serving gourmet treats, Ximending is a food lover's paradise.

4. Endless Entertainment: Enjoy a movie at the historic Shin Shin Theater, a blend of old-world charm and modernity. Visit themed cafes, sing your heart out at karaoke bars, or test your skills at a claw machine arcade. The district also features live music venues and street performers that add to its lively atmosphere.

5. Nightlife Hub: As the sun sets, Ximending comes alive with a vibrant nightlife. Whether you're drawn to bars with live music, energetic clubs, or late-night street food, there's something for every night owl.

Exploring Ximending

Start your journey at the iconic Red House, a historical building now serving as a cultural center with exhibitions and events. Navigate through the mazelike pedestrian zone to discover hidden gems and must-see shops, including the famous "No Name Street," a hotspot for fashionistas. Don't miss trying local favorites like bubble tea and the distinct taste of stinky tofu. Catch a movie at the Shin Shin Theater, where history and modern cinema meet. Test your luck at a claw machine arcade, a quintessential Ximending experience. As evening falls, dive into the district's dynamic nightlife, where the excitement never wanes.

Tips for Your Ximending Visit

1. Wear comfortable shoes to easily navigate the bustling streets.
2. Practise your bargaining skills at street vendors and select shops.
3. Carry cash for street food and smaller stores.
4. Use public transport, with convenient access to Ximending via the Ximen and Beimen MRT stations.

* * *

Tamsui Old Street

Located along the peaceful banks of the Tamsui River at the northwestern edge of Taipei, Tamsui Old Street (; Dànshuǐ Lǎojiē) invites visitors on a nostalgic journey through history. Dating back to the 18th century, Tamsui Old Street was a significant trading hub during the Qing Dynasty. The historical atmosphere is still evident in the architecture and cultural traditions that continue to thrive in the area.

Culinary Journey

Prepare for a delightful food adventure as you explore Tamsui Old Street's vibrant street food scene. Savor local specialties like Ah-Gei (fried stinky tofu) and irresistible fish balls. Indulge in traditional snacks, candied fruits, or the famous "iron eggs," each bite reflecting the street's rich culinary heritage.

Shopping Extravaganza

Get lost in the winding alleys filled with shops offering a variety of souvenirs and handmade goods. Discover unique trinkets, ornate tea sets, and clothing with a distinct Taiwanese charm. Enjoy haggling for the perfect souvenir to remember your visit.

Cultural Highlights

Stroll among historic buildings that blend Chinese and Japanese architectural styles. Admire the intricate designs of temples such as Mizuhiro Jinja and the Tamsui Presbyterian Church, showcasing the district's diverse cultural influences.

Riverside Relaxation

Take a leisurely walk along the scenic Tamsui Riverwalk, enjoying panoramic views of the river. Feel the cool breeze as you observe the lively atmosphere along the riverbanks. You might also consider taking a ferry across to Bali District, a quaint fishing village, or simply relaxing by the water with a refreshing drink.

Sunset Splendor

End your day at Tamsui Old Street by witnessing a breathtaking sunset. Watch as the sky transforms into a canvas of warm colours, casting a golden glow over the tranquil Tamsui River, a magical moment you won't soon forget.

Tips for Your Visit

1. Getting There: Take the MRT red line from Taipei Main Station to Tamsui Station for easy access to Tamsui Old Street.

2. Operating Hours: Most shops and eateries are open from late morning to late evening, giving you plenty of time to explore.

3. Weather Considerations: Keep in mind the humid climate, especially in summer. Dress comfortably and apply sunscreen during daytime visits.

4. Cash on Hand: While some places accept credit cards, it's wise to carry cash, particularly for street vendors and smaller shops.

Chapter 4: Culinary Delights

Traditional Taiwanese Cuisine

Taipei's culinary landscape is a delightful mix of high-end dining and the vibrant energy of night markets. At its heart lies traditional Taiwanese cuisine, a harmonious blend of indigenous flavors, Chinese culinary heritage, and Japanese influences. Here's a guide to must-try dishes, where to find them, and what to expect in terms of cost:

Noodles

1. Beef Noodle Soup (NT$100-200): This iconic dish features a rich, aromatic broth, tender beef, and perfectly cooked noodles, often topped with pickled mustard greens.

- Where to Try: Lin Dong Fang Beef Noodle Soup, Niu Ba Ba.

2. Lu Rou Fan (Braised Pork Belly over Rice) (NT$50-100): A comfort food favourite, Lu Rou Fan consists of melt-in-your-mouth pork belly braised in a savoury soy sauce blend, served over steamed rice.

- Where to Try: Wu Shan Liang Pork Ribs Soup, Yong Kang Street.

Snacks and Dumplings

1. Gua Bao (Taiwanese Hamburger) (NT$50-80): These soft steamed buns are stuffed with braised pork belly, pickled vegetables, crushed peanuts, and cilantro.

- Where to Try: Liu Dian Night Market, Feng Chia Night Market.

2. Xiao Long Bao (Soup Dumplings) (NT$100-150 per basket): Delicate dumplings filled with savoury pork and broth, a must-try for dumpling lovers.

- Where to Try: Din Tai Fung, Din Yuan Xiao Long Bao.

Other Delights

1. Stinky Tofu (NT$50-70 per skewer): Despite its strong smell, this deep-fried fermented tofu, served with a pungent sauce and pickled veggies, is a Taipei classic.

- Where to Try: Shilin Night Market, Raohe Street Night Market.

2. Beef Hot Pot (NT$300-500+ per person): Ideal for sharing, this dish involves simmering a pot of broth with an assortment of meats, vegetables, noodles, and dumplings.

- Where to Try: Mala Hotpot, Mongolian Hot Pot Paradise.

* * *

Night Markets and Street Food

Taipei's night markets are a treasure trove for food enthusiasts. These bustling, open-air markets are not only a sensory delight but also offer a variety of affordable street food that showcases the city's vibrant culinary culture.

Night Market Must-Tries (Prices are approximate)
Classics (NT$50-100 or $1.50-3 USD)
1. Stinky Tofu: A daring choice, deep-fried fermented tofu with a distinctive aroma and surprisingly creamy texture.

2. Bubble Tea: A Taiwanese beverage staple, with a wide range of flavours and toppings.

3. Gua Bao (Taiwanese Hamburger): A delicious steamed bun filled with braised pork or other savoury ingredients.

4. Oyster Omelette: A savoury dish featuring plump oysters, eggs, and vegetables, topped with a tangy sauce.

5. Grilled Squid: Skewered and grilled squid, basted with sweet or savoury sauces.

Snacks and Skewers (NT$30-80 or $1-2.50 USD)
1. Tempura: Lightly battered and fried vegetables and seafood, crispy and flavorful.

2. Dan Bing (Scallion Pancake): A savoury pancake filled with eggs, scallions, and sometimes additional fillings like vegetables or meat.

3. Chicken or Pork Skewers: Marinated, grilled skewers perfect for a quick and satisfying snack.

Heartier Options (NT$100-200 or $3-6 USD)

1. Beef Noodle Soup:A warming bowl of noodles in rich beef broth, often with braised beef slices and vegetables.

2. Lu Rou Fan (Braised Pork Rice): Tender, flavorful braised pork belly served over steamed rice, a comforting Taiwanese classic.

3. Yong Tau Foo: Tofu puffs and vegetables stuffed with savoury fillings, simmered in a tasty broth.

Popular Night Markets

1. Shilin Night Market: The largest and most famous night market, offering a wide range of food and shopping options.

   • Location: Shilin District, accessible by MRT.
   • Tip: Prices may be slightly higher due to its popularity with tourists.

2. Raohe Street Night Market: A bustling market with a strong focus on Taiwanese street food.

   • Location: Songshan District, accessible by MRT.

3. Ningxia Night Market: A smaller, more local market, balancing food stalls and shopping.

   • Location: Datong District, accessible by MRT.

4. Tonghua Night Market (Linjiang Street): Known for its trendy snacks and comforting traditional Taiwanese dishes.

- Location: Da'an District, accessible by MRT.

5. Huaxi Street Night Market (Snake Alley): Famous for its snake dishes and other unique local delicacies.

- Location: Wanhua District, accessible by MRT.

Tips for Navigating Night Markets
1. Cash is King: Most vendors prefer cash payments.

2. Arrive Hungry: With so many options, you'll want to try a little of everything!

3. Point and Order: If you're unsure how to order, pointing at what you want is perfectly acceptable.

4. Bargain: Negotiation is expected, especially for non-food items.

5. Embrace the Adventure: Be open to trying new flavours and dishes you may not find elsewhere.

Additional Notes
1. Operating Hours: Night markets usually run from late afternoon (around 5 pm) to late night (around 1 am).

2. Prices: The prices listed are rough estimates and may vary depending on the market, vendor, and portion size.

Exploring Taipei's traditional cuisine and night markets is an essential part of experiencing the city's rich cultural tapestry. Each dish tells a story, and every market offers a unique glimpse into the vibrant heart of Taipei.

* * *

Fine Dining Experiences in Taipei

Amidst the dynamic street markets and bustling food stalls of Taipei lies an elevated world of fine dining that caters to those in search of culinary sophistication and elegance. For diners with refined palates, Taipei's fine dining scene offers a remarkable blend of artistry, flavor, and atmosphere, promising an evening of indulgence and sensory delight.

Culinary Highlights

1. French Haute Cuisine with a Taiwanese Twist: Michelin-starred venues like L'Atelier de Joel Robuchon bring French culinary excellence to Taipei, where classic techniques are infused with local Taiwanese flavours. Each dish is crafted with meticulous precision, offering a luxurious fusion of East and West.

2. Modern Interpretation of Traditional Flavors: At RAW by Andre Chiang visionary chef Andre Chiang deconstructs and reimagines Taiwanese cuisine. Expect to encounter playful, avant-garde presentations and inventive takes on familiar flavours, making for a dining experience that is both nostalgic and new.

3. Globally Inspired Gastronomy: Restaurants like MUME offers a modern European dining experience with a global perspective. Here, international techniques meet seasonal Taiwanese ingredients, resulting in unique dishes that reflect a harmonious blend of global influences and local produce.

A Night of Sensory Delights

Fine dining in Taipei is more than just a meal, it's an immersive experience that engages all the senses:

1. Impeccable Service: Guests can anticipate attentive and polished service from start to finish. The knowledgeable staff is adept at guiding diners through the menu, answering questions, and ensuring that each aspect of the dining experience is seamless and satisfying.

2. Exquisite Presentation: Every element of the dining experience is visually stunning, from the intricately plated dishes to the elegant table settings. The aesthetic appeal of the food is complemented by the ambiance of the restaurant, creating a feast for the eyes as well as the palate.

3. Ambiance Matters: The ambiance in Taipei's fine dining venues ranges from romantic, dimly lit settings to modern spaces with panoramic skyline views. Each restaurant offers a carefully curated atmosphere that enhances the overall dining experience.

Planning Your Fine Dining Sojourn

1. Reservations are Essential: Securing a table at Taipei's most sought-after fine dining establishments often requires booking well in advance. Reservations can typically be made online or through your hotel concierge, ensuring you don't miss out on the experience.

2. Dress Code: While not all restaurants enforce a strict dress code, smart attire is recommended. Consider wearing something elegant, such as a refined outfit or cocktail dress, to complement the upscale setting.

3. Budget Considerations: Fine dining in Taipei commands higher prices compared to casual dining options. Be sure to budget accordingly when planning your itinerary, and consider these experiences as a special indulgence during your visit.

Exploring Local Ingredients

Taipei's fine dining scene is celebrated for its use of fresh, seasonal ingredients sourced from local farms and artisans. Diners can expect to encounter an array of distinctive Taiwanese produce and premium ingredients that reflect the island's rich agricultural heritage:

1. Seasonal Seafood: Many fine dining restaurants in Taipei highlight the island's premium seafood, featuring dishes with wild-caught fish, plump oysters, and other fresh catches that showcase the bounty of the surrounding waters.

2. High-Quality Meats: Diners can enjoy beautifully marbled beef, tender poultry, and locally sourced pork, each prepared with skill and artistry to highlight their natural flavours.

3. Exotic Vegetables: Taiwanese vegetables, such as baby bok choy, snow peas, and a variety of seasonal mushrooms, are often featured in dishes, offering a taste of the island's unique and vibrant produce.

For those looking to indulge in the sophisticated side of Taipei's culinary scene, fine dining provides a memorable experience where local ingredients meet international techniques in a setting of elegance and refinement. Whether you're celebrating a special occasion or simply seeking to explore the culinary heights of the city, Taipei's fine dining establishments are sure to impress.

* * *

Vegetarian and Vegan Options in Taipei

Taipei's culinary landscape is a paradise for vegetarians and vegans, offering a diverse array of delectable, wallet-friendly options. From fine dining establishments to bustling night markets, the city caters to plant-based diets with an impressive range of choices.

Vegetarian and Vegan Eateries
   1. Fine Dining: Upscale vegetarian fare is available at some of Taipei's high-end establishments, where innovative dishes and sophisticated settings are the norm. Expect to spend between NTD$500-1000+ (US$16-33+) per person.

2. BaganHood (Xinyi District): A trendy spot known for its international vegetarian dishes, including plant-based burgers and pizzas. The chic ambiance adds to the dining experience, with meals typically costing NTD$700-1000 (US$23-33+) per person.

3. Miss Green (Daan District & Dunhua District): Specialises in veganized Western comfort food, offering vegan burgers, salads, and pastas. Prices range between NTD$350-500 (US$11-16+) per person.

4. Casual Fare: For more laid-back dining, Taipei offers numerous vegetarian and vegan joints where flavorful and affordable options are plentiful. Anticipate spending around NTD$100-300 (US$3-10+) per person.

Notable Spots
   1. Vege Creek (Multiple Locations): Known for customizable vegan noodle bowls with fresh vegetables and mock meats.

2. Hoshina (Daan District): Offers Taiwanese vegetarian classics like three-cup "chicken" and hearty noodle soups.

3. Three To Vegetarian Restaurant (Zhongzheng District): A local favourite

for Taiwanese vegetarian staples at budget-friendly prices.

Night Market Delights

Vegetarian Stalls: Taipei's night markets also cater to vegetarians and vegans with a variety of plant-based dishes like gluten seitan and mushroom creations. Dishes typically cost between NTD$50-150 (US$2-5+).

Notable Markets

1. Shilin Night Market: Known for its vegetarian stinky tofu among other vegetarian delights.

2. Raohe Street Night Market: Features dedicated vegetarian stalls offering vegan-friendly options like scallion pancakes.

Pro Tips

1. Look for Signs: The green "" (sù) character indicates vegetarian options, while "" (quán sù) signifies vegan options. Many places offer English menus or visual aids.

2. Use Apps: Utilise apps like HappyCow to find nearby vegetarian and vegan eateries.

3. Ask Locals: Locals are often happy to recommend hidden gems, so don't hesitate to ask for suggestions!

Beyond the Plate

1. Coffee Shops: Many cafes in Taipei offer plant-based milk alternatives like soy, oat, and almond milk.

2. Bakeries: While fully vegan bakeries are rare, some offer vegan pastries. Look for signs or ask about ingredients.

* * *

Coffee Culture and Tea Houses in Taipei

Taipei's rich culinary tapestry extends beyond food, embracing a vibrant coffee culture and a deeply rooted tea tradition, providing a serene contrast to the city's energetic atmosphere.

Coffee Culture

1. Independent Cafes: These cafes offer distinct atmospheres and a focus on quality, featuring locally roasted beans and artisanal brewing methods like pour-over and cold brew. Expect to pay NTD$120-200 (US$4-7) for a latte or cappuccino.

  • Notable Areas: Daan District, Shida Night Market, and Yongkang Street.

2. Chain Cafes: From global giants like Starbucks to local favourites like 85°C and Cama Café, these chains offer familiar drinks at lower prices. Lattes and cappuccinos generally cost NTD$80-150 (US$3-5).

3. Specialty Coffee Shops: For discerning coffee enthusiasts, specialty coffee shops showcase single-origin beans crafted by skilled baristas. Prices are higher, ranging from NTD$150-250 (US$5-8) or more.

Tea Houses

1. Traditional Teahouses: These serene spaces often feature low tables, tatami mats, and elaborate tea sets. Guests can participate in tea ceremonies, where loose-leaf teas are brewed and shared. Prices vary depending on the tea selection and ceremony, typically costing NTD$200-500 (US$7-18) per

person.

- Notable Areas: Dihua Street and Dadaocheng are renowned for traditional tea houses.

2. Modern Tea Bars: These venues offer a contemporary take on tea culture, with inventive tea blends, fruit-infused options, and tea lattes. Prices range from NTD$100-200 (US$3-7).

Tips

1. Pairing: Many cafes and tea houses offer pastries, cakes, and light bites to complement your drinks.

2. Souvenirs: Consider purchasing loose-leaf teas or tea sets as mementos of your Taipei experience.

3. Minimum Spend: Some traditional tea houses may have minimum spending requirements, so be mindful of that.

4. Ask for Advice: If you're new to tea culture, don't hesitate to ask staff for guidance on tea varieties and brewing techniques.

Taipei's vegetarian, vegan, coffee, and tea scenes offer an eclectic mix of flavours and experiences, making it a city that truly caters to all tastes and preferences.

Chapter 5: Culture

Temples and Shrines in Taipei

T aipei is a city deeply rooted in tradition, where temples and shrines stand as pillars of its cultural heritage. These sacred sites are not only places of worship but also reflect the spiritual and historical essence of the city.

Buddhist Gems

1. Longshan Temple: One of Taipei's most iconic temples, Longshan Temple beautifully combines Buddhist and Taoist elements. Built in 1738, it's dedicated to Guanyin, the Goddess of Mercy. The temple's intricate carvings and vibrant decorations create a serene ambiance, making it a must-visit for anyone interested in history and culture. The temple is known for its ornate dragon columns, detailed woodwork, and the peaceful central courtyard where visitors often engage in prayer or meditation.

2. Linchi Monastery: Located in Beitou district, Linchi Monastery is a serene retreat founded in 1900. It embodies the principles of Japanese Zen Buddhism with its minimalist architecture and tranquil gardens, offering a peaceful escape from the bustling city. The monastery's simplicity and natural surroundings make it an ideal spot for quiet reflection and meditation.

Taoist Treasures

1. Xingtian Temple: Xingtian Temple is dedicated to Guan Yu, a revered warrior god who symbolises loyalty and righteousness. This temple is particularly popular among businessmen and police officers who come seeking blessings for success and protection. The temple's striking architecture and vibrant colours make it a lively place of worship. Visitors can witness traditional Taoist rituals and offerings, adding a dynamic layer to the cultural experience.

2. Dalongdong Baoan Temple: Dating back to the 18th century, Dalongdong Baoan Temple is dedicated to Mazu, the Goddess of the Sea. The temple is a historical treasure, known for its intricate carvings, traditional courtyards, and the captivating ambiance that reflects centuries of Taiwanese belief and culture. The temple frequently hosts traditional performances and ceremonies, allowing visitors to immerse themselves in local traditions.

Beyond Buddhism and Taoism

Xiahai City God Temple: A smaller but significant temple, Xiahai City God Temple is dedicated to the City God, who is believed to protect the city's well-being. This temple offers a unique glimpse into Taiwanese folk religion, where visitors can participate in fortune-telling rituals and observe local customs. The temple is particularly known for its matchmaking rituals, making it a popular spot for singles seeking divine intervention in their love lives.

Temple Etiquette and Tips

1. Dress Modestly: Ensure your attire is respectful, covering shoulders and knees.

2. Observe Rituals Quietly: Maintain a respectful silence during ongoing rituals and ceremonies.

3. Offerings: Some temples allow visitors to make offerings, such as incense or vegetarian food, as a sign of respect.

4. Photography: Always seek permission before taking photos, especially during religious ceremonies or in sacred areas.

Visiting these temples and shrines offers more than just a visual feast, it's an opportunity to connect with the spiritual and cultural heartbeat of Taipei.

* * *

Museums and Art Galleries in Taipei

Taipei is a haven for art and history enthusiasts, boasting an impressive array of museums and galleries that showcase the city's rich cultural heritage and vibrant artistic scene.

Museums

1. National Palace Museum: Housing one of the world's finest collections of Chinese imperial artefacts, the National Palace Museum is a must-visit. The museum's collection includes exquisite jade carvings, ancient bronzes, intricate porcelains, and timeless paintings, offering a comprehensive overview of Chinese art and history.

- Location: No. 22 Zhongshan N. Rd., Sec. 1, Zhongzheng District, Taipei City 100001, Taiwan
- Entry Fee: TWD$250

2. Taipei Fine Arts Museum (TFAM): TFAM is the heart of Taipei's modern and contemporary art scene, showcasing works from Taiwanese and international artists. The museum hosts rotating exhibitions that span a wide range of

styles and mediums, making each visit a unique experience.

- Location: 181 Zhongshan N. Rd., Sec. 3, Zhongzheng District, Taipei City 100003, Taiwan
- Entry Fee: TWD$180

3. Museum of Contemporary Art Taipei (MOCA): MOCA is a dynamic space dedicated to contemporary art, featuring installations, video art, and multimedia works. The museum's exhibitions often challenge conventional boundaries, making it a hub for innovative and thought-provoking art.

- Location: No. 39 Chang-An W. Rd., Sec. 1, Zhongzheng District, Taipei City 100013, Taiwan
- Entry Fee: TWD$250

4. National Taiwan Museum: As Taiwan's oldest museum, the National Taiwan Museum offers a deep dive into the island's natural history, anthropology, and archaeology. The museum's exhibits highlight Taiwan's indigenous cultures, diverse ecosystems, and geological wonders.

- Location: No. 228, Sec. 1, Zhongshan N. Rd., Zhongzheng District, Taipei City 100001, Taiwan
- Entry Fee: Free

5. Shung Ye Museum of Formosan Aborigines: Dedicated to preserving the heritage of Taiwan's indigenous tribes, this museum offers a rich exploration of their traditions, art, and way of life. The exhibits feature everything from traditional clothing to ceremonial artefacts.

- Location: No. 2, Yumen St., Xinyi District, Taipei City 11060, Taiwan

· Entry Fee: TWD$150

Art Galleries

1. Eslite Gallery: Located alongside the renowned Eslite bookstore, this gallery specialises in modern and contemporary Chinese art, featuring works by both established and emerging artists. The gallery's exhibitions often explore themes related to greater China and its cultural evolution.

- Location: No. 245, Sec. 4, Zhongxiao E. Rd., Daan District, Taipei City 10691, Taiwan

2. Chi-Wen Gallery: Known for its focus on photography and video art, Chi-Wen Gallery showcases cutting-edge works by Taiwanese and international artists. The gallery is a platform for visual expression that pushes the boundaries of contemporary art.

- Location: No. 32, Ln. 2, Sec. 6, Zhongshan N. Rd., Shilin District, Taipei City 11145, Taiwan

3. Tina Keng Gallery: Specialising in contemporary Asian art, Tina Keng Gallery features a diverse range of artistic styles and mediums. The gallery represents both established and mid-career artists, making it a key player in the Asian art scene.

- Location: No. 15, Ln. 70, Sec. 1, Dunhua S. Rd., Daan District, Taipei City 10691, Taiwan

4. Aki Gallery: Aki Gallery is dedicated to supporting emerging Taiwanese artists, offering a space for works that challenge traditional perspectives.

The gallery's exhibitions often provoke thought and encourage dialogue on contemporary issues.

- Location: No. 7, Ln. 70, Sec. 1, Dunhua S. Rd., Daan District, Taipei City 10691, Taiwan

5. VT Art Salon: VT Art Salon focuses on emerging talent from Taiwan and Southeast Asia, showcasing fresh and innovative artistic expressions across various mediums. The gallery is known for its vibrant and dynamic exhibitions that highlight new voices in the art world.

- Location: B1, No. 17, Ln. 56, Sec. 4, Renai Rd., Daan District, Taipei City 10690, Taiwan

Whether you're drawn to the ancient artifacts of the National Palace Museum or the contemporary creations in Taipei's cutting-edge galleries, the city's cultural institutions offer something to inspire every visitor.

* * *

Performing Arts and Theater in Taipei

Taipei's performing arts scene is a vibrant reflection of the city's cultural diversity, offering everything from traditional operas to avant-garde theatre. Visitors can immerse themselves in a range of performances that showcase both the rich traditions and the contemporary creativity of Taiwan.

Major Performing Arts Centers

1. Taipei Performing Arts Center (TPAC): TPAC is a modern architectural marvel that houses three distinct theatres: the Grand Theater, Multi-form Theater, and Proscenium Playhouse. Each venue hosts a variety of performances, including operas, musicals, dance shows, plays, and puppet performances, offering something for every artistic taste.

- Location: Shilin District, Taipei City (Closest MRT Station: Jiantan)
- Operation Hours: Generally 12 pm – 9 pm
- Entry Fees: Varies depending on the performance.

2. National Theater and Concert Hall (NTCH): Situated within the Chiang Kai-shek Memorial Hall complex, NTCH is one of Taipei's most prestigious cultural venues. It regularly hosts classical music concerts, operas, dance performances, and theatrical productions by both local and international artists.

- Location: Zhongzheng District, Taipei City (Closest MRT Station: Chiang Kai-shek Memorial Hall)
- Operation Hours: Generally 11:30 am – 9 pm
- Entry Fees: Varies depending on the performance.

Traditional Theatre

1. The National Theater: Located in Ximending, The National Theater is a historic venue dedicated to traditional Taiwanese performing arts. It offers a cultural deep dive into Taiwan's rich heritage with performances of traditional opera, puppetry, and folk dances.

- Location: Ximending District, Taipei City (Closest MRT Station: Ximen)
- Operation Hours: Generally 10 am – 5 pm (closed Mondays)
- Entry Fees: Varies depending on the performance.

2. Lee Tang Hua Puppet Theatre: This theatre is dedicated to the art of Taiwanese puppetry, a cherished cultural tradition. Located in Datong District, it offers captivating puppet shows that are popular with both locals and visitors.

- Location: Datong District, Taipei City (Closest MRT Station: Beimen)
- Operation Hours: Performances usually on weekends and holidays.
- Entry Fees: Varies depending on the performance.

Tips for Attending Performances

1. Ticket Purchase: Buy tickets online or at the box office in advance, especially for popular shows.

2. Language Considerations: Some venues may offer subtitles or English-language programs, so check ahead if language is a concern.

3. Dress Code: Smart casual is typically the expected attire.

4. Arrival Time: Arrive early to find good seats and settle in before the show begins.

* * *

Traditional Festivals and Events in Taipei

Taipei's calendar is filled with vibrant traditional festivals that provide insight into the city's rich cultural and spiritual life. From the bustling celebrations of Lunar New Year to the tranquil reverence of the Qingming Festival, these events offer a unique window into Taiwanese traditions.

Spring Festivals

1. Lunar New Year (Late January - Early February): The most significant festival in Taiwan, Lunar New Year is celebrated with a week-long series of events including firecracker displays, temple visits, family reunions, and lion dances. The entire city comes alive with decorations and festivities.

- Dates: Varies each year based on the lunar calendar, generally falls in late January or early February.
- Tip: Book accommodation well in advance as this is a peak travel season.

2. Lantern Festival (15th Day of the First Lunar Month - February/Early March): The Lantern Festival marks the end of Lunar New Year celebrations. The highlight is the release of thousands of lanterns into the night sky, each carrying wishes for the coming year. Lantern displays can be found throughout the city.

- Dates: Varies each year, typically falls in February or early March.

Summer Festivals

1. Qingming Festival (Tomb-Sweeping Day) (Early April): Qingming is a time to honour ancestors, with families visiting cemeteries to clean gravestones and make offerings of food, tea, and incense. It's a solemn but significant cultural event.

- Dates: Typically falls on April 5th each year.

2. Dragon Boat Festival (5th Day of the Fifth Lunar Month - Late May/June): This vibrant festival commemorates the ancient poet Qu Yuan with dragon boat races held on the Tamsui River. The energetic atmosphere is accompanied by traditional drumming and the enjoyment of zongzi (rice dumplings).

- Dates: Varies annually based on the lunar calendar, typically falls in late May or June.

Autumn Festivals

1. Mid-Autumn Festival (Moon Festival) (15th Day of the Eighth Lunar Month - September): The Mid-Autumn Festival celebrates family and the harvest with mooncake tasting and beautiful lantern displays. It's a time for reunions and reflecting on the year.

- Dates: Varies annually based on the lunar calendar, typically falls in September.

2. Double Tenth National Day (October 10th): Celebrating the founding of the Republic of China, Double Tenth Day features parades, military displays, and fireworks, with festivities held across the city.

- Dates: October 10th each year.

Beyond the Major Festivals

Temple Festivals: Throughout the year, various temples in Taipei hold festivals in honour of their patron deities. These events often feature lively parades, lion dances, and traditional music, providing a glimpse into local religious practices.

Tips for Experiencing Traditional Festivals

1. Research: Learn about the customs and traditions associated with each festival to fully appreciate the significance of the events.

2. Dress Comfortably: Be prepared for crowds and, during summer festivals, hot weather.

3. Cash is King: Smaller vendors at festivals may not accept credit cards, so carry some cash for food and souvenirs.

4. Embrace the Experience: Engage with the local culture, ask questions, and immerse yourself in the festivities.

Attending these traditional festivals and events will deepen your appreciation for Taipei's cultural heritage and create lasting memories of your visit to this vibrant city.

Chapter 6: Unravelling Taipei's History

Colonial Influences in Taipei

U nveiling Taipei's Colonial Legacy (1895-1945)
Taipei's transformation from a small trading post to a bustling metropolis is deeply tied to the period of Japanese colonial rule (1895-1945). Although this era was marked by both challenges and complexities, the enduring impact of Japanese influence on Taipei's urban planning, infrastructure, and cultural identity is evident.

Transformation and Modernization

Urban Development and Infrastructure: Under Japanese rule, Taipei under-went a significant modernization process, evolving from dispersed villages into a well-planned city. The introduction of a grid street system, the con-struction of neoclassical public buildings, and the establishment of essential infrastructure like sewage and water systems were key to this transformation. Iconic landmarks, such as the Governor-General's Office (now the Presidential Office) and Taipei Railway Station, stand as lasting reminders of this era.

Economic Expansion

Focus on Industry and Trade: Japan's emphasis on industrialization spurred the growth of factories and trade in Taipei. This economic drive attracted migrants seeking job opportunities, leading to a rapid increase in the city's population.

Education and Cultural Influence

1. Modern Education System: The Japanese implemented a modern education system, founding schools and universities that significantly raised literacy rates and cultivated a more educated population. Institutions like National Taiwan University, established during this time, remain central to Taipei's academic environment.

2. Cultural Preservation and Assimilation: While promoting Japanese culture, efforts were also made to preserve aspects of Taiwanese heritage, such as renovating temples and documenting indigenous cultures. However, it's important to note that these efforts often aligned with the broader agenda of Japanese colonial control.

Architectural Heritage

Japanese Architectural Styles: The influence of Japanese architecture is visible in structures like the National Taiwan Museum, with its characteristic red brick facade, and the Botanical Garden, which was designed in traditional Japanese landscape style. These landmarks contribute a unique aspect to Taipei's architectural landscape.

A Complex Legacy

The legacy of Japanese colonialism in Taiwan is a topic of ongoing debate. While the period brought modernization and infrastructure development, it was also marked by the suppression of Taiwanese culture and identity.

Exploring Colonial Influences

1. National Taiwan Museum: This museum features exhibits that explore Taiwan's history during the Japanese colonial period, showcasing artefacts and documents from that time.

2. Botanical Garden: Enjoy a peaceful walk through this garden, which reflects

Japanese landscape design principles.

3. Taipei Railway Station: A historic landmark from the Japanese era, this station remains a vital transportation hub and a symbol of Taipei's colonial past.

Modern Taiwan's Development

Post-War Transformation of Modern Taiwan

After World War II and Taiwan's return to Chinese control in 1945, Taipei began a remarkable transformation into the vibrant city it is today. Here's an overview of the key factors driving this change:

Land Reform and Industrialization (1950s-1960s)

The KMT government implemented widespread land reforms, redistributing land to farmers, which empowered rural communities and boosted agricultural productivity. Concurrently, a push for industrialization led to the growth of key sectors like textiles, electronics, and shipbuilding, supported by skilled labor and government incentives, setting the stage for Taiwan's economic rise.

The Taiwan Miracle (1970s-1990s)

The 1970s and 1980s saw extraordinary economic growth, often referred to as the "Taiwan Miracle." This boom was driven by significant foreign investment, export-focused growth strategies, heavy investment in education, and the expansion of small and medium enterprises (SMEs), particularly in technology.

Emergence of High-Tech and Globalisation (1990s-Present)

As the global economy shifted towards high-tech industries, Taiwan became a leader in semiconductor production, establishing itself as a major player in computer chip manufacturing. Taiwan's entry into the World Trade Organization (WTO) in 2002 further integrated its economy globally, enhancing market access for Taiwanese exports.

Challenges and Future Prospects

Despite its impressive achievements, Taiwan faces current challenges, including increasing competition from China, growing income inequality, and unresolved political tensions with mainland China. Looking forward, Taiwan is focused on advancing its high-tech industry, promoting innovation, and diversifying its economy, with a growing emphasis on sustainable development and green technology.

Taipei serves as a symbol of Taiwan's incredible progress, with its modern infrastructure, thriving financial sector, and dynamic tech scene. From the towering Taipei 101 to the numerous tech startups throughout the city, Taipei reflects the nation's journey toward progress and prosperity.

Chapter 7: Outdoor Adventures

Hiking Trails and Nature Parks

Taipei surprises many with its abundant natural beauty. Beyond the bustling city streets lies a landscape rich with mountains, volcanic areas, rejuvenating hot springs, and lush forests, all waiting to be explored. So, put on your hiking boots and get ready to discover Taipei's hidden gems!

Hiking Trails

1. Yangmingshan National Park: This park embodies Taipei's outdoor charm, offering a variety of trails for all skill levels. Here, you can hike through volcanic landscapes, enjoy seasonal flower displays, and take in breathtaking views of the city. Notable trails include:

- Mount Qixing Main Peak: A moderately challenging hike that rewards you with stunning summit views.
- Lengshuikeng Hiking Trail: A scenic route ideal for spotting waterfalls and enjoying green vistas.
- Small Guanyin Mountain: A more accessible trail perfect for families and casual hikers, featuring scenic overlooks.
- Elephant Mountain (Xiangshan Hiking Trail): A short but rewarding hike with panoramic views of the city, including the iconic Taipei 101. Be

prepared for stair climbs and crowds, especially on weekends.

2. Jiantanshan Hiking Trail: This trail takes you through dense forests, leading to a viewing platform with spectacular city views. It offers a moderate challenge and a peaceful escape from the urban environment.

3. Neihu Ridge Trail: Discover a network of hidden trails offering scenic views and the chance to stumble upon secluded temples and shrines. For a tranquil retreat, head to Thumb Mountain (Muzhi Shan) and 95 Peak (Jiuwu Feng).

4. Qixing Mountain Hiking Trails: This trail system accommodates various difficulty levels and provides stunning vistas. Whether you explore the historic Qixing Main Peak Trail or tackle the steeper Nursery Line Trail, you're in for an exciting adventure.

Nature Parks
1. Fuyang Eco Park: A green oasis within the city, this park offers scenic trails, perfect for picnics and a relaxing day in nature's embrace.

2. Guandu Nature Park: This wetland sanctuary is home to a diverse array of bird species. Stroll along the waterfront trails, observe migratory birds, and soak in the peacefulness of nature.

3. 140 Height Park: Located atop a hill, this park offers sweeping views of the city and the Keelung River. Whether you hike or bike to the summit, you'll enjoy a refreshing workout and stunning cityscapes.

Tips for Hiking in Taipei
1. Select trails that match your fitness level and the challenge you seek.

2. Research trail details, including length, elevation gain, and estimated duration, to plan your hike.

3. Bring essentials like sturdy hiking shoes, sunscreen, insect repellent, water, and snacks.

4. Check the weather forecast to prepare for rain or extreme temperatures.

5. Practise environmental responsibility by sticking to designated trails and leaving no trace.

* * *

Hot Springs and Spa Retreats

Taipei, Taiwan's vibrant capital, may not be the first place you think of for a peaceful spa retreat. Yet, nestled among the city's energetic atmosphere and towering buildings are serene havens offering unique opportunities to unwind and rejuvenate with hot springs and spa treatments.

The Appeal of Hot Springs: Nature's Therapy

Taiwan is rich in geothermal activity, and Taipei is situated at the edge of this volcanic zone. Hot springs, known as "wenquan" () in Mandarin, have been cherished for their healing properties for centuries.

The Benefits of Hot Springs

1. Relaxation and Stress Relief: The warm, mineral-rich waters are excellent for soothing tired muscles and calming the mind.

2. Improved Circulation: The heat enhances blood flow, leaving you feeling rejuvenated and energised.

3. Pain Relief: A soak in these waters can help alleviate joint pain and stiffness.

4. Skin Benefits: The minerals in the water nourish the skin, promoting a healthy complexion.

Popular Hot Spring Resorts Near Taipei

1. Beitou Hot Springs: Just a short trip from Taipei City, this historic resort town offers a variety of public and private hot spring facilities. You can enjoy traditional Japanese-style outdoor baths (rotenburo) or indulge in luxurious spas with modern amenities.

2. Wulai Hot Springs: Located in a picturesque setting of mountains and rivers, Wulai offers a more rustic hot spring experience. Many resorts here incorporate indigenous Taiwanese elements into their design and treatments.

Choosing Your Hot Spring Experience

1. Public vs. Private: Public bathhouses offer a more affordable option with communal pools, while private facilities provide more privacy and often include extras like massages and saunas.

2. Day Trips vs. Overnight Stays: You can opt for a day pass to enjoy a few hours of hot spring relaxation, or choose an overnight stay for a more immersive spa retreat experience.

Taipei also boasts a range of top-quality spas offering a wide variety of treatments designed to rejuvenate your body and spirit. These tranquil sanctuaries provide a perfect escape from the city's hustle and bustle.

Treatments to Consider

1. Traditional Chinese Medicine: Experience ancient healing practices like acupuncture, cupping therapy, and herbal massages.

2. Relaxation Massages: Treat yourself to different massage styles, from deep tissue to aromatherapy.

3. Beauty Treatments: Refresh your skin with facials, body scrubs, and other pampering services.

Finding the Perfect Spa

1. Luxury vs. Boutique: Choose between luxurious five-star spas with extensive treatment options or boutique spas that offer personalised experiences.

2. Theme-Based Spas: Discover unique spa experiences inspired by Taiwanese tea ceremonies or indigenous cultural traditions.

While hot springs and spa treatments are the main attractions, these retreats often offer additional activities to enhance your stay:

1. Hiking: Many hot spring resorts are set in scenic landscapes, making them ideal for a pre- or post-soak hike.

2. Cultural Experiences: Visit nearby temples, explore local villages, or participate in traditional tea ceremonies.

3. Fine Dining: After a relaxing spa session, indulge in delicious local cuisine.

Important Tips

1. Swimwear: Bring a swimsuit and comfortable slippers for both hot spring and spa visits.

2. Etiquette: Respect local customs in public hot springs, such as keeping quiet and showering before entering the pools.

3. Reservations: Especially during weekends and holidays, it's a good idea to book your hot spring or spa experience in advance.

* * *

Cycling Routes

Taipei invites cyclists to explore its extensive network of bike paths, perfect for experiencing the city's diverse landscapes at your own pace. Whether you're an experienced rider or prefer a leisurely pace, Taipei has a route for everyone. Here's your comprehensive guide to cycling in Taipei:

Must-Try Cycling Routes

1. Riverside Routes: Enjoy cycling free from car traffic along Taipei's scenic riverside paths, including:

- Xindian River Trail (Ximen to Gongguan): Follow the Xindian River, taking in captivating views of the city and lush surroundings. This mostly flat route is suitable for cyclists of all skill levels.

- Keelung River Bicycle Path: Ride along the Keelung River, catching glimpses of Taipei's outskirts and natural beauty, with some moderate inclines along the way.

- Dahan River Left Bank Bike Path: Escape the urban hustle and immerse yourself in nature's tranquillity as you pedal along the peaceful Dahan River.

2. Urban Exploration: Easily navigate Taipei's city centre with these accessible routes:

- Taipei City Cycling Map: Explore various districts like Daan, Wenshan, and Shilin via designated bike lanes.

- The Roosevelt Bike Path: Experience the heart of the city on this short yet scenic route, offering views of historical landmarks and vibrant neighbourhoods.

3. Nature Escapes: Embark on an adventure through Taipei's natural landscapes with these cycling options:

- Elephant Mountain Hiking Trail: Combine your ride with a short hike for panoramic views of the city atop Elephant Mountain.

- Yangmingshan National Park: Cycle through designated paths within the park, where you'll encounter volcanic landscapes, hot springs, and colourful gardens though be ready for some hilly terrain.

Tips for Cycling in Taipei

1. Bike Rentals: Numerous shops offer hourly or daily rentals, while bike-sharing programs provide convenient options throughout the city.

2. Safety First: Always prioritise safety by wearing a helmet and following traffic rules. Be mindful of pedestrians and maintain a safe distance from vehicles.

3. Etiquette on Shared Paths: Show courtesy to pedestrians and fellow cyclists by signalling your presence with a bell and exercising caution, especially in crowded areas.

4. Essential Gear: Bring sunscreen, a water bottle, and comfortable clothing. Consider a bike lock for securing your bike when it's unattended.

Beyond the City Limits

1. Tamsui Old Street: Enjoy a scenic ride along the riverfront to Tamsui Old Street, known for its historic charm and delicious seafood.

2. Jiufen: Head to the enchanting mountain town of Jiufen, famous for its narrow alleyways, traditional teahouses, and stunning views.

Resources for Cyclists

1. Taipei City Cycling Map: Download cycling maps from the Taipei City Cycling website for easy navigation.

2. YouBike: Utilise Taipei's bike-sharing program for convenient cycling options throughout the city.

* * *

Water Activities and Beaches

Although Taipei isn't famous for its coastlines, it surprises visitors with a range of water-based adventures and beachside relaxation opportunities. Here's a guide to experiencing Taipei's aquatic activities:

Water Activities

1. Stand-Up Paddleboarding (SUP): Experience the city from a new perspective by trying SUP at Bitan Scenic Area or Pinglin Riverside Park. Rentals and lessons are often available for beginners.

2. Kayaking and Canoeing: Enjoy a peaceful paddle along the Keelung River or explore the mangroves of Danshui River. Various companies offer guided tours and equipment rentals, making it easy to get started.

3. Snorkelling: Discover the underwater world at Waiao Beach in Jinshan District, where unique black volcanic rock formations create an intriguing snorkelling spot. Seasonal rentals and guided tours may be available for enthusiasts.

Beaches

Though not all of Taipei's beaches are ideal for swimming due to strong currents or rocky shores, they provide excellent spots for sunbathing and enjoying the coastal scenery. Here are some notable options:

1. Baishawan Beach (): Located in Xinyi District, this beach offers golden sands, designated swimming areas (depending on conditions), and nearby dining options.

2. Wanli Beach (): Found in Wanli District, this beach features stunning rock formations and is popular among surfers and windsurfers (conditions permitting). Swimming may be restricted due to strong currents.

3. Fulong Beach (): North of Taipei, Fulong Beach offers sandy shores, swimming areas (when conditions are favourable), and opportunities for surfing and bodyboarding (conditions permitting).

4. Jinshan Beach (): Situated in Jinshan District, this beach boasts golden sands and picturesque mountain views. Swimming may be limited due to currents, but it's a serene retreat near the famous Jinshan Hot Springs.

Important Tips

1. Always check beach safety conditions before swimming, as lifeguards may not be present at all locations.

2. Be cautious of strong currents and riptides, especially at Wanli Beach and Fulong Beach.

3. Most beaches are accessible by public transport, though some may require a combination of trains and buses. Taxis are also readily available.

4. Pack essentials like sunscreen, a hat, sunglasses, and appropriate swimwear.

5. Consider bringing water shoes for navigating rocky shorelines.

6. Show respect for the environment by disposing of waste properly.

Chapter 8: Shopping and Entertainment

Shopping Districts and Markets

Taipei is a shopper's paradise, offering a vibrant mix of luxury malls, bustling night markets, and charming boutiques tucked away in alleyways. Whether you're searching for high-end brands, unique souvenirs, or the latest fashion trends, Taipei has something for every style and budget. Here's your complete guide to navigating Taipei's diverse shopping scene:

High-End Shopping

1. Xinyi District: Indulge in luxury shopping at Taipei 101 and nearby malls like ATT 4 FUN, Bellavita, and Breeze Center, where flagship stores of international brands and designer boutiques await.

2. Zhongxiao Dunhua: Experience sophistication at upscale department stores like SOGO Fuxing, alongside chic boutiques scattered throughout the area.

Trendy Boutiques and Independent Stores

1. Ximending: Dive into the youthful energy of Ximending, filled with indie clothing stores, quirky accessory shops, and stylish footwear outlets. Don't miss the cultural hotspot of Red House for unique designs and art galleries.

2. Gongguan Night Market: Popular among students, this market offers trendy

and affordable clothing, accessories, and cosmetics, making it a great place to spot local fashion trends.

Night Markets

1. Shilin Night Market: Taipei's most famous night market, offering an array of clothing, electronics, souvenirs, and mouth-watering street food.

2. Raohe Street Night Market: Step into tradition at this historic market, where you can savour authentic Taiwanese snacks while browsing clothing and accessory stalls.

3. Ningxia Road Night Market: A haven for food lovers, this late-night market is packed with Taiwanese delicacies, along with a variety of clothing vendors.

Specialty Markets

1. Dihua Street: Immerse yourself in history on this quaint street, lined with shops selling dried goods, medicinal herbs, teas, and traditional Chinese crafts.

2. Tianmu Market Place: Discover a weekend treasure trove of secondhand goods and vintage finds, where haggling adds to the authentic shopping experience.

Beyond Shopping Malls

1. Department Stores: Taiwanese department stores are more than just shopping destinations; they also offer dining, cafes, and entertainment, making them perfect for leisurely exploration.

2. Independent Boutiques: Venture off the beaten path to discover hidden gems in Taipei's alleyways, where you'll find handmade crafts, local designer apparel, and niche specialty shops.

While bargaining is uncommon in high-end stores, it's a common practice at night markets and independent shops. Start with a friendly negotiation and enjoy the exchange.

Most shopping districts and malls are easily accessible via public transport, and many stores accept major credit cards. However, carrying cash is advisable, especially for smaller shops and night market vendors.

* * *

Entertainment Venues and Nightlife

Taipei's nightlife is vibrant and diverse, offering something for everyone, whether you're a fan of live music or looking to dance the night away.

Live Music Venues

1. Legacy (Various Locations): A major player in Taipei's music scene, Legacy hosts both local and international acts at multiple locations. Cover charges vary, with hours generally running from 8 pm until late.

2. Revolver (Zhongzheng District): This lively bar and music venue offers a wide selection of international craft beers, tasty nachos, and regular live music events. Entry is free on weekdays, with a small cover charge on weekends. Operating hours are from 6:30 pm to 3 am (Thursday-Tuesday) and 6:30 pm to 4 am (Friday-Saturday).

3. Blue Note Taipei (Da'an District): Immerse yourself in jazz at this elegant venue, where renowned international and local jazz artists perform. Entry fees vary, with showtimes typically from 8 pm to midnight (Thursday-Sunday), and closed on Tuesdays.

Nightclubs

1. OMNI (Xinyi District): This upscale nightclub delivers an immersive experience with cutting-edge sound systems and stunning light displays, featuring EDM sets by top DJs. Entry fees vary, with hours extending from 10 pm to 4 am (Thursday-Sunday).

2. Korner (Xinyi District): Known for its underground techno and house music, Korner has relocated but retained its vibrant atmosphere. Entry fees are reasonable and often include a complimentary drink. The club usually operates from 10 pm to 4 am (Friday-Saturday).

Other Entertainment Options

1. KTV (Karaoke): Embrace a beloved Taiwanese tradition by visiting one of the many KTV bars around the city. Rent a private room, sing your heart out, and enjoy snacks and drinks. Prices vary depending on room size and time. Most KTVs operate late into the night, with some open 24/7.

2. Rooftop Bars: Enjoy breathtaking city views while sipping cocktails at one of Taipei's chic rooftop bars. Entry fees may apply, with operating hours typically starting in the late afternoon and extending into the night.

Important Notes

Always check entry fees and operating hours, as they can change. It's a good idea to visit the venue's website or social media for the latest updates.

Additional Tips

1. Consider getting a Taipei EasyCard for seamless access to public transportation, including late-night buses.

2. Many venues offer drink specials and happy hour discounts, especially on weekdays.

3. Dress codes vary by venue, with upscale clubs often enforcing stricter attire

compared to casual pubs and music spots.

4. Prioritise safety and stay alert, particularly during late-night outings.

* * *

Unique Souvenirs and Local Crafts

If you want to bring home a piece of Taipei's charm, delve into the world of unique souvenirs and local crafts that truly capture the essence of your journey.

Celebrate Taiwanese Crafts

1. Ceramics and Porcelain: Head to Yingge District, often dubbed "Taiwan's Jingdezhen," where you'll find an array of exquisite ceramics. From fine tableware to decorative pieces and miniature replicas of landmarks, there's something for every taste.

2. Indigenous Crafts: Experience the rich cultural heritage of Taiwan's indigenous tribes by exploring handcrafted items like intricately woven textiles, beaded jewellery, and hand-carved wooden sculptures, each reflecting traditional craftsmanship.

3. Lacquerware: Appreciate the detailed artistry of Taiwanese lacquerware, with its elaborate designs layered onto wood or bamboo. You'll find beautiful boxes, trays, and even chopsticks, all showcasing this traditional art form.

Beyond Ordinary Souvenirs

1. Ri Xing Character Moulds: Step back in time at the Ri Xing Printing House & Museum, the last place in Taipei where traditional block printing thrives. Pick

up character printing blocks bearing words like "love," "peace," or "hope" for a truly unique keepsake.

2. Paper Umbrellas and Lanterns: Bring a touch of Taiwanese charm to your home with colourful paper umbrellas and lanterns. Available in various sizes and designs, these items add a whimsical flair to any space.

3. Tea Sets and Accessories: Immerse yourself in Taiwan's tea culture by purchasing beautifully crafted tea sets made from porcelain or ceramic. Specialty shops offer an array of tea-related accessories, including strainers, warming teapots, and elegant tea caddies.

Where to Find the Perfect Souvenirs

1. Night Markets: Soak up the vibrant atmosphere of Taipei's night markets, where you'll discover an abundance of treasures, from jade trinkets to quirky phone cases adorned with Taiwanese mascots.

2. Dihua Street: Wander through the historic charm of Dihua Street, where traditional shops and modern boutiques offer an enticing mix of silk scarves, teapots, and bamboo creations.

3. Department Stores: For a more curated shopping experience, visit Taipei's upscale department stores like Taipei 101 Mall, which feature local crafts and designer pieces infused with Taiwanese motifs.

Insider Tips

1. Haggling: Bargaining is a common practice at night markets and smaller shops. Approach with respect and aim for a fair price.

2. Material Matters: Choose natural fabrics like silk or cotton, and ensure wood or bamboo items are sustainably sourced.

3. Support Local Artisans: Look for shops and markets that support local

artisans. Not only will you find unique items, but you'll also be contributing to the local community.

Chapter 9: Day Trips and Excursions

Jiufen and Pingxi: A Journey into Taiwan's Past

E scape Taipei's vibrant energy and venture into the serene, historical towns of Jiufen and Pingxi. Nestled in the scenic mountains just beyond the city, these villages offer a rich glimpse into Taiwan's cultural heritage, breathtaking landscapes, and unique traditions.

Jiufen: A Nostalgic Experience

Known as the "Gold Rush Town," Jiufen flourished during the Japanese colonial era due to its gold mining industry. Today, it still exudes a nostalgic charm with its narrow, winding streets lined with traditional tea houses, quaint shops, and cozy eateries. A leisurely walk through these atmospheric alleys feels like a journey back in time.

Stunning Views: Perched on a mountainside, Jiufen provides stunning panoramic views of the coastline and surrounding hills. Whether you're gazing at Keelung Harbor or Teapot Mountain, the scenery is captivating both during the day and under the twinkling city lights at night.

Gastronomic Adventures: Jiufen is a haven for food lovers, offering a wide variety of delectable treats. Be sure to try the town's signature dish, "Taro Balls in Peanut Soup," for a comforting treat. The lively night market is also a must-visit, where you can sample local specialties like stinky tofu, oyster omelettes, and Taiwanese sausages. And don't forget to enjoy a cup of fragrant Taiwanese tea amidst the vibrant atmosphere.

Anime Inspiration: The famous Studio Ghibli film "Spirited Away" drew inspiration from Jiufen's unique architecture and traditional tea houses. Explore iconic spots like the A-Mei Teahouse and immerse yourself in the town's connection to pop culture.

Getting to Jiufen: From Taipei Main Station, take a train to Ruifang Station, then catch a bus or taxi to Jiufen Old Street.

Pingxi: The Magic of Lanterns

Lantern Wonderland: Set in lush, green valleys, Pingxi is renowned for its enchanting sky lantern festival. Throughout the year, especially during the Lantern Festival, visitors gather to release colourful lanterns bearing their wishes and prayers, creating a magical display in the night sky.

Historical Significance: Pingxi's history is deeply rooted in its gold mining past. Visit the Pingxi Coal Mine Museum and stroll through the historic Shifen Old Street, lined with traditional shops and eateries.

Scenic Train Ride: Experience a scenic journey aboard the Pingxi Branch Line, a historic railway that offers breathtaking views of mountains, rivers, and charming villages. Capture picturesque moments as the train winds through tunnels and crosses bridges, adding to the allure of exploring Pingxi.

Shifen Waterfall: For a natural retreat, visit the nearby Shifen Waterfall, a beautiful cascade surrounded by lush greenery. Enjoy a peaceful walk along the trails or simply relax in this refreshing escape from city life.

Getting to Pingxi: Like Jiufen, take a train from Taipei Main Station to Ruifang Station, then transfer to Pingxi Station via the Pingxi Branch Line.

Jiufen and Pingxi: A Combined Adventure

Since these two villages are close to each other, you can easily visit both in a single day. Start your day exploring Jiufen's historical streets and sampling local delicacies. In the afternoon, head to Pingxi to soak in its charming atmosphere and enjoy a unique railway journey. As the day ends, you might witness the captivating sight of sky lanterns illuminating the night sky, depending on the season.

Seasonal Note

The sky lantern festival in Pingxi occurs throughout the year, with peak celebrations during the Lantern Festival. Jiufen's weather can be unpredictable, so be ready for either sunshine or rain.

* * *

Tamsui and Fisherman's Wharf: A Coastal Escape from Taipei

A trip to Taipei isn't complete without exploring beyond the city centre. Tamsui, situated at the mouth of the Tamsui River, offers a charming district full of history, culinary delights, and stunning waterfront views. Here's how to make the most of your visit to Tamsui and its neighbouring Fisherman's Wharf:

Tamsui Old Street

A Glimpse into the Past: Stroll through Tamsui Old Street, where narrow lanes are lined with traditional shops selling a variety of souvenirs, local crafts, and delicious street food. Pass under the iconic red archway at the entrance and immerse yourself in the nostalgic atmosphere.

Culinary Pleasures: Tamsui Old Street is a food lover's paradise. Indulge in Ah-Gei, the district's signature dish, a tasty fried glutinous rice ball with savoury or sweet fillings. Don't miss out on local favourites like oyster omelettes, grilled squid, and the famous "iron eggs," a unique local delicacy with a distinctive taste and texture.

Cultural Gems: Amidst the lively streets, discover historical treasures such as the well-preserved Mizuhiro Main Store, a relic from the Japanese colonial period, and the stately Tamsui Customs House, a reminder of the district's rich trading history.

Tamsui Fisherman's Wharf

Peaceful Views: Just a short trip from Tamsui Old Street, Tamsui Fisherman's Wharf offers a tranquil retreat. Stroll along the waterfront promenade, enjoying sweeping views of the Tamsui River and the distant Guanyin Mountain.

Relaxing Activities: Take a leisurely boat ride along the Tamsui River, where you'll be treated to stunning views of the city skyline and the iconic Tamsui Lover's Bridge. Learn about the area's maritime history at the informative Fisherman's Wharf Visitor Center.

Sunset Magic: End your day by witnessing the breathtaking sunset at Tamsui Fisherman's Wharf. As the sky is painted in fiery hues, capture the moment and soak in the romantic ambiance.

Getting There

Easy Access: Tamsui is easily accessible from Taipei City via the MRT red line to Tamsui Station. From there, you can take a leisurely walk to Tamsui Old Street or a quick 10-minute bus ride to Fisherman's Wharf.

Additional Tips

1. Wear comfortable shoes, as exploring Tamsui involves a lot of walking.
2. Bring an umbrella, especially during the rainy season from May to September.
3. Engage in polite bargaining at the shops along Tamsui Old Street.
4. Carry some cash, as some vendors might still prefer cash transactions.

Enhance your Tamsui visit by combining it with other day trips from Taipei City. Consider visiting Jiufen, known for its tea houses and nostalgic charm, or exploring Keelung, a coastal city with historical sites and delicious seafood.

* * *

Wulai Indigenous Village

Nestled in the lush mountains just south of Taipei, Wulai District offers a peaceful getaway from the city's fast pace. This captivating area is known for its stunning natural scenery, rejuvenating hot springs, and deep cultural heritage rooted in the Atayal people, one of Taiwan's indigenous groups.

Experience Atayal Culture

- Dive into Tradition: Wulai invites you to immerse yourself in the rich culture of the Atayal people. A visit to the Wulai Atayal Museum provides insight into their history, traditions, and way of life. Enjoy mesmerising performances of traditional dances and music, and appreciate the craftsmanship of their intricate handicrafts.

- Discover the Wulai Waterfall: Set off on a scenic hike along well-kept trails to the impressive Wulai Waterfall. Feel the cool mist and enjoy the tranquil surroundings as you take in the beauty of nature.

Relaxation and Rejuvenation

Soothe Your Senses in Hot Springs: Wulai is famous for its natural hot springs, which are believed to have healing properties. You can choose from various public hot spring resorts or opt for a more luxurious experience at private hot spring hotels, catering to different preferences and budgets.

Adventure Activities

1. Wulai Scenic Train Ride: Enjoy a delightful ride on the Wulai Scenic Train, a charming narrow-gauge railway that winds through the mountains, offering panoramic views of the valley and lush forests.

2. Explore Nature Trails: Put on your hiking boots and explore Wulai's scenic trails. Whether you're aiming for the summit of Wulai Mountain for sweeping views or prefer a leisurely stroll along the riverside, there's a trail suited for every type of adventurer.

3. Taste of Atayal Cuisine: Wulai tempts you with the unique flavours of Atayal cuisine. Enjoy dishes like bamboo shoot soup, grilled mountain meats, and wild vegetables. Don't miss the "Qilu" millet cake, a sweet treat that's sure to delight.

Planning Your Wulai Visit

Wulai is about an hour away from Taipei by bus or train, making it an ideal day trip. For a deeper experience, consider staying overnight to fully appreciate the peaceful ambiance.

As you explore Wulai, respect the local culture and traditions. Dress modestly when visiting temples and be mindful of photography etiquette, especially when engaging with indigenous communities.

* * *

Yehliu Geopark

Take an unforgettable trip beyond Taipei City to Yehliu Geopark, located along the northeast coast. This geological wonderland, shaped by thousands of years of wind, waves, and weathering, showcases an array of unique rock formations, each telling its own fascinating story.

Marvel at the Geological Wonders of Yehliu Geopark

1. Mushroom Rocks: These iconic formations, resembling giant mushrooms, are among the park's most popular attractions.

2. Queen's Head: Don't miss the park's most famous landmark, a rock formation sculpted by nature to resemble a queen's head. Be prepared for a short wait to snap a photo, as it's a favourite spot for visitors!

3. Honeycomb Rocks: Observe the captivating honeycomb patterns etched into these rocks, showcasing the effects of erosion on softer rock layers.

4. Candle Rocks: Marvel at the slender, candle-like formations that stand at various angles, carved by the forces of nature.

5. Fairy's Shoe: Let your imagination run wild with the delicate rock formation that looks like a fairy's shoe, a whimsical creation sure to enchant visitors.

Exploring Yehliu Geopark

The park is divided into three sections, each offering a unique exploration experience along the dramatic coastline:

1. Section 1: Encounter the park's most famous formations, including the Queen's Head, Mushroom Rocks, and Fairy's Shoe.

2. Section 2: Venture deeper to discover stunning seascapes and formations like Dragon Head and Peanut Rock.

3. Section 3: Explore peaceful coves, sea caves, and vibrant tide pools filled with marine life in this quieter area.

Planning Your Visit

1. Getting There: Yehliu Geopark is about an hour's drive from Taipei City. Public buses and taxis are readily available for easy access.

2. Opening Hours: The park is open daily from 8:30 AM to 5:30 PM.

3. Admission Fees: A small entrance fee allows you to explore the park's wonders.

4. Time Required: Plan to spend 2-3 hours exploring the park's captivating landscapes. Be sure to wear sturdy shoes for navigating the uneven terrain.

5. Sun Protection: Bring sun protection, as there's limited shade throughout the park.

Explore More in the Area

1. Fresh Seafood: Enjoy delicious fresh seafood at the coastal restaurants near the park entrance.

2. Yehliu Geopark Visitor Center: Learn more about the park's geological features and history at the visitor centre.

3. Souvenir Shops: Browse for unique souvenirs and local crafts inspired by the park's remarkable formations.

Chapter 10: Practical Information

Accommodation Options in Taipei

Taipei offers a wide range of lodging choices to suit different budgets and preferences. Here's a guide to help you find the perfect place to stay:

Luxury (NT$8,000+ per night)

1. Mandarin Oriental Taipei (Xinyi District): Experience unparalleled luxury with stunning city views, exceptional service, and fine dining.

2. The Regent Taipei (Zhongshan District): Enjoy opulent surroundings, Michelin-starred dining, and a rejuvenating spa in the heart of the city.

3. Fairmont Taipei (Xinyi District): Delight in impressive views, spacious rooms, and top-tier service in this premium hotel.

Mid-Range (NT$3,000 - NT$8,000 per night)

1. W Taipei (Xinyi District): This trendy hotel offers a vibrant atmosphere, stylish bars, and a prime location for exploring the city.

2. The Sherwood Taipei (Neihu District): Featuring modern comfort and elegant design, this hotel offers spacious rooms, excellent amenities, and easy access to the MRT.

3. Linsen Living (Zhongshan District): A boutique hotel blending comfort and style, with well-appointed rooms and a central location near major attractions.

Budget-Friendly (Under NT$3,000 per night)

1. Myrtree Taipei (Ximending District): Enjoy the lively Ximending area at this trendy hostel offering clean dorms and private rooms at reasonable rates.

2. Walker Hostel (Main Station District): A conveniently located hostel with cosy beds, communal spaces, and easy access to public transport.

3. Vienna House Easy Taipei (Songshan District): A modern, clean hostel close to Songshan Airport, providing comfortable and affordable accommodation.

Unique Experiences

1. Beitou Hot Spring Hotels (Beitou District): Experience traditional Taiwanese hospitality at a ryokan or hotel with access to natural hot springs. Prices vary based on amenities.

2. Homestays: For a deeper cultural experience, consider a homestay to see Taiwanese family life up close. Rates usually start at NT$2,000 per night.

Choosing the Right Accommodation

Besides the options listed, Taipei has many other hotels, hostels, and Airbnbs to fit various budgets and preferences. Consider factors such as location, amenities, and online reviews. Booking in advance is recommended, especially during peak seasons.

* * *

Language and Communication in Taipei

Effective communication can enhance your experience in Taipei. Here's a quick guide to help you navigate language barriers:

Official Language

Mandarin Chinese is the official language spoken throughout Taipei.

English Proficiency

You'll find English signs at major tourist spots, metro stations, and some restaurants. Many younger locals know basic English phrases.

Essential Mandarin Phrases

Learning a few key phrases can be very helpful:

- Hello (Nǐ hǎo):
- Thank you (Xiè xie):
- Please (Qǐngwèn):
- Excuse me (Duì bù qǐ):
- How much is this? (Zhè ge duōshǎo qián?):
- Do you speak English? (Nín shuō yīngwén ma?):

Communication Apps

Use translation apps like Google Translate or Pleco to help with language barriers. These apps often provide voice and camera translations for signs and menus.

Body Language

In Taiwanese culture, non-verbal cues such as nodding or a slight bow are common ways to show respect. Smiling can also help create a positive interaction.

Gestures

Be mindful of certain gestures, as they may have different meanings. When in doubt, use verbal communication.

Business Cards

In professional settings, exchanging business cards is customary. Having bilingual cards can be useful for meetings.

Helpful Resources

Consider carrying a Mandarin phrasebook for additional vocabulary and pronunciation help. Many hotels offer concierge services to assist with communication.

* * *

Currency and Money Matters

Currency

The official currency in Taiwan is the New Taiwan Dollar (NT$), also abbreviated as TWD. Bills come in NT$2,000, NT$1,000, NT$500, NT$200, and NT$100, while coins are available in NT$50, NT$20, NT$10, NT$5, and NT$1.

Exchanging Your Currency

You can exchange foreign currency for NT$ at the airport or various locations in the city:

1. Banks: Offer competitive rates but have limited hours (typically 9:00 am to 3:30 pm on weekdays).

2. Foreign Exchange Bureaus: Available with longer hours, though rates might be slightly less favourable. Look for signs like "Bureau De Change," "Geld Wechseln," or "Cambio."

3. ATMs: Convenient for withdrawing cash using debit or credit cards. Be aware of potential fees from both your bank and the ATM operator.

Tips for Exchanging Money
  1. Research exchange rates beforehand to ensure a fair rate.

2. Carry both cash and credit cards. While credit cards are widely accepted, having cash is handy for smaller places and public transport.

3. Keep receipts from exchanges as they may be needed for converting leftover NT$ back to your home currency.

4. Be cautious with money changers offering "zero fees," as they may offer less favourable rates.

Additional Money Matters
  1. Tipping: Not customary in Taipei, but a small tip for exceptional service is appreciated.

2. Bargaining: Common at night markets and some independent shops, but always negotiate respectfully.

3. Taxes: Prices usually include a 5% value-added tax (VAT).

* * *

Safety Tips and Emergency Contacts

Taipei is known for its safety and low crime rates, but it's always wise to stay alert. Here are some key safety tips and emergency contacts to help you during your stay:

Safety Tips

1. Stay Aware: Keep an eye on your surroundings, especially in busy areas. Be cautious with your belongings, particularly bags and wallets.

2. Be Careful in Crowded Areas: Watch out for pickpockets, especially in bustling night markets and on public transport. Avoid carrying large amounts of cash and secure your valuables.

3. Pedestrian Safety: Be cautious when crossing streets, even at crosswalks. Pedestrians may not always have the right of way, particularly with scooters around. Use designated crossings and stay vigilant. Consider wearing reflective gear at night for better visibility.

4. Use Licensed Transportation: Choose licensed taxis with visible metres and avoid unregistered taxis or unofficial ride-sharing services.

5. Prepare for Natural Disasters: Taiwan is prone to earthquakes and occasional typhoons. Familiarise yourself with your hotel's evacuation procedures and locate nearby emergency shelters. Consider travel insurance that covers natural disasters.

Emergency Contacts

1. Police: Call 110 for police assistance.

2. Fire and Ambulance: Dial 119 for fire emergencies, medical help, or ambulance services.

3. English Emergency Line: Reach 0800-024-111 for 24/7 English-language assistance and interpretation during emergencies and other situations.

4. Taipei City Government Hotline: Call 1999 for various non-emergency assistance.

5. Foreign Affairs Police (English-speaking): Contact 02-2556-6007 for support or if you encounter criminal incidents.

Additional Recommendations

1. Learn Basic Mandarin: While English is increasingly common, knowing a few Mandarin phrases can be very helpful.

2. Get Travel Insurance: Ensure you have travel insurance for medical emergencies, lost belongings, or travel disruptions.

3. Download Emergency Apps: Use apps like "Taiwan Subway Navigation" and "MAPS.ME" for translations, directions, or connecting with local authorities.

* * *

Useful Mandarin Phrases

Learning some Mandarin phrases can enhance your experience in Taipei. Here are key expressions:

Greetings and Politeness

· Hello (informal): Nǐ hǎo ()
· Hello (formal): Nín hǎo ()

- Thank you: Xiè xiè ()
- You're welcome: Bú kè qi ()
- Excuse me / I'm sorry: Duì bù qǐ ()
- I don't understand: Wǒ bù míng bái ()
- May I see someone who can help me?: Wǒ kěyǐ jiàn dào kěyǐ bāng wǒ de rén ma ()

Numbers

- One: Yī ()
- Two: Èr ()
- Three: Sān ()
- Four: Sì ()
- Five: Wǔ ()
- Six: Liù ()
- Seven: Qī ()
- Eight: Bā ()
- Nine: Jiǔ ()
- Ten: Shí ()

Directions

- Left: Zuǒ biān ()
- Right: Yòu biān ()
- Front: Qián ()
- Back: Hòu ()
- Go straight: Zhí ()
- Toilet: Wèi shēng jiān ()

Food and Dining

- Can I reserve a table?: Wǒ kěyǐ yùdìng yī zhāng zhuō zi ma ()
- Menu: Cài dān ()
- Excuse me, I have dietary restrictions: Duì bù qǐ, wǒ yǒu yǐn shí jìn zhǐ ()
- Taste: Wèi dào ()
- Spicy: Là ()
- Not spicy: Bù là ()

Transportation

- Take the subway: Zuò dì tiě ()
- Take the bus: Zuò bā shì ()
- Airport: Jī chǎng ()
- How much is this?: Zhè gè duō shǎo qián ()

Shopping

- Can I take a look?: Wǒ kěyǐ kàn yī kàn ma ()
- How much is this?: Duō shǎo qián ()
- Can it be a bit cheaper?: Kěyǐ pián yī diǎn ma ()

Additional Advice

1. Pronunciation: It might be challenging, but locals appreciate your effort to speak Mandarin.

2. Phrasebook or App: Carry a phrasebook or use a translation app for complex situations.

3. Gestures: Use them to complement your phrases.

4. Local Customs: Observe local customs, such as a slight bow as a sign of

respect.

Conclusion

As you embark on your Taipei adventure, may this guidebook be your trusted companion, leading you through the vibrant streets, bustling markets, and tranquil temples of this captivating city.

But your journey doesn't stop here! To keep the magic of Taipei alive, consider these suggestions:

1. Capture Memories: Document your experiences with photos, videos, or a travel journal. Share these on social media to inspire others to explore Taipei's wonders.

2. Leave Reviews: Help fellow travellers by writing honest reviews on your favourite restaurants, attractions, and hidden gems. Your insights will enhance others' experiences.

3. Immerse Yourself in Local Culture: Connect with locals by learning basic Mandarin phrases and supporting independent businesses and cultural events. Share your appreciation for Taiwanese culture with friends and family.

4. Plan Your Return: Taipei's dynamic nature means there's always something new to discover. Start dreaming about your next visit, whether it's exploring Sun Moon Lake or venturing to Kaohsiung.

By sharing your adventures, you join a global community of travellers and inspire others to explore the beauty of Taipei and Taiwan.

We hope this guidebook has enriched your experience and created lasting memories. May your journey be filled with culinary delights, cultural encounters, and a deep appreciation for this vibrant city.

Travel safely, embrace curiosity, and keep the spirit of Taipei alive in your heart!

Made in United States
Troutdale, OR
12/23/2024

27192553R00066